Thomas Thellusson Carter, John William Kempe

Reservation of the Blessed Sacrament for the sick and dying

Not inconsistent with the order of the Church of England

Thomas Thellusson Carter, John William Kempe

Reservation of the Blessed Sacrament for the sick and dying
Not inconsistent with the order of the Church of England

ISBN/EAN: 9783337259457

Printed in Europe, USA, Canada, Australia, Japan

Cover: Foto ©ninafisch / pixelio.de

More available books at **www.hansebooks.com**

RESERVATION

OF THE

BLESSED SACRAMENT

FOR THE SICK AND DYING

Not inconsistent with the Order of the
Church of England

BY THE

REV. J. W. KEMPE, M.A.

OF UNIVERSITY COLLEGE, DURHAM

ASSISTANT CURATE AND PRECENTOR OF S. JOHN THE DIVINE, KENNINGTON
SOMETIME ASSISTANT CURATE OF S. OSWALD'S, DURHAM, AND
CHAPLAIN OF THE SOUTH WESTERN HOSPITAL

WITH PREFACE BY THE

REV. T. T. CARTER, M.A.

HON. CANON OF CHRIST CHURCH, OXFORD, AND WARDEN OF
THE HOUSE OF MERCY, CLEWER

PUBLISHED BY REQUEST

London

G. J. PALMER, 32, LITTLE QUEEN STREET

LINCOLN'S INN FIELDS

1887

To the Reverend
THOMAS THELLUSSON CARTER, M.A.

*Hon. Canon of Christ Church, Oxford;
Warden of the House of Mercy, Clewer; and Superior-General of the
Confraternity of the Blessed Sacrament.*

TO you, my dear Superior-General, I dedicate this Treatise, in grateful acknowledgment of all that you have done by the persuasiveness and consistency of your example (if I may venture thus to speak) no less than by the clearness of your dogmatic teaching, in commending Eucharistic Truth and Worship to the people of England; also, in dutiful recognition of that paternal interest with which during the past quarter of a century you have presided over the extending organisation of the Confraternity of the Blessed Sacrament, in which some 13,000 communicants are now enrolled; and in token of my appreciation of your personal kindness in thus linking my name with your own, by introducing to the notice of Churchmen the following considerations respecting the "Restoration of the primitive custom of reserving the Blessed Sacrament for the sick and dying," which during so many years has been specially remembered in our prayers.

> I remain, my dear Sir,
> With great respect,
> Ever yours affectionately,
> JOHN WILLIAM KEMPE.

S. JOHN THE DIVINE, KENNINGTON,
Easter, 1887.

TABLE OF CONTENTS.

	PAGE
PREFACE	ix—xv
CHAP. I. INTRODUCTION	1—6

CHAP. II. RESERVATION OF THE EUCHARIST CONSISTENT WITH ANGLICAN FORMULARIES.
Historical considerations respecting (1) the sixth Post-communion rubric; (2) the Order for the Communion of the sick; (3) the Twenty-eighth Article of Religion . . . . 7—20

CHAP. III. RESERVATION OF THE EUCHARIST RECOGNISED IN THE BOOK OF COMMON PRAYER.
Recognition of the usage of Reservation in (1) the Ornaments rubric; (2) the Preface concerning Ceremonies, originally prefixed to the Book of 1549, as justifying Ceremonies therein retained; (3) the rubric preceding the Post-communion in the Eucharistic Office.
This rubric examined (i) historically, (ii) liturgically, (iii) in its relation to the Post-communion . . . 21—46

CHAP. IV. RESERVATION OF THE EUCHARIST ENJOINED BY THE ECCLESIASTICAL LAW OF ENGLAND.
Considerations respecting (1) the authority of the Provincial Constitutions and Commentaries of Lyndwood; (2) the Constitution of Archbp. Peccham (which has never been repealed) regarded in its (i) historical, (ii) legal, (iii) liturgical bearings; (3) the Second-part of this Constitution, directing that the Eucharist be carried to the sick with due reverence 47—107

			PAGE
CHAP. V.	OF COMMUNION UNDER BOTH KINDS. Considered in its (1) theological, (2) historical, (3) practical bearings.		108—130
CHAP. VI.	SUMMARY AND CONCLUSION. Concerning (1) ill-advised action either in forbidding or restoring Reservation; (2) the due observance of the sixth Post-communion rubric; (3) the liturgical recognition of the principle of Reservation; (4) the Order for the Communion of the sick and the evidence of Bishop Sparrow; (5) the Latin Prayer-book of 1560; (6) the practical result of preceding considerations		131—186

PREFACE.

It was inevitable that, sooner or later, the subject-matter of this Treatise should become a leading thought at this present time. The revival of Church doctrine and of Church use of late years has been grounded on a belief in primitive Catholic tradition; and there is no usage, no point of practice, more certainly primitive or Catholic than the "Reservation of the Blessed Sacrament for the sick and dying"; and it is one that cannot lightly be put aside as not concerning the deepest interests of the soul's life. We have every certainty that history can supply that it was not the principle of the English Reformation to disparage, or dispossess us of, any usage which could claim such authority or plead such necessity. It would be a waste of time to seek to prove this, whatever may be thought of the consequences flowing from such considerations.

That the custom has all but entirely dropped out of use is hardly a sufficient argument that its disuse was intended. Other customs had been entirely dropped amongst us which are now generally accepted as truly and legitimately our proper inheritance. Reservation for the sick is but one of several portions of the sacramental system of the Church which have been subjected to a temporary eclipse but have happily emerged into light, and now in so many cases every day more and more prevailing. That it has been preserved in the sister Church of Scotland is a point in favour of such Reservation among us, which other customs, now generally accepted, do not possess.

The publication of the following Treatise is not the first occasion on which this question has been mooted, though never before has it been so carefully and elaborately discussed as to its historical, liturgical, and canonical authority in the Church of England. Beside other appeals for its restoration, many may remember Robert Brett's earnest representations to Convocation of the blessing it would confer in numberless cases, of which he, as a medical man, had personal experience. It is, I believe, an open secret, that Bishop Wilberforce would have done his best to forward this petition but for the fear lest the authoritative restoration of this custom should, in the then first fervour of the Ritual movement, lead on to practices which the Church of England has never recognised, and which, even in former ages, were not observed in her Communion. Cases are well known where episcopal sanction has been given for such Reservation under special circumstances. But what is generally felt, and felt more and more deeply, is this :—that such cases are not, and cannot be, merely special. Valuable as our provision is for private Communion, and greatly as it would naturally be preferred where time and circumstances of place and sufficient bodily strength permit, yet the cases are innumerable where the sick chamber, or the bedside in a many-peopled chamber, among our poor, or in our hospitals, is entirely unsuitable for any reverent Celebration of the Divine Mysteries, or where extreme sickness or imminent death render more than one or two prayers altogether impracticable. And is nothing to be allowed to hard-worked priests in populous parishes, especially at the greater festivals?

Or is no regard to be paid to the increasing tendency to observe the old Catholic rule of Fasting Communion, where priests are liable at any time of day or night, it may be in the midst of a meal, to be suddenly called out to communicate a dying parishioner? Everywhere of late years earnest endeavours have been made to do away the reproach of a non-communicating people,—endeavours which are now being abundantly blest. To make such arrangements that the *Viaticum* should be easily and readily obtained by the poorest and most suffering of our people in our dense population is the natural—is it not the necessary?—outcome of a happily growing tendency to respond to such endeavours.

The argument sure to be raised, and already alluded to, of the risk of Reservation for the sick, if authorised, leading on to Reservation for merely devotional purposes, touches on an important principle. Hooker's reasoning against allowing the fear of possible consequences to hinder a legitimate use was important in his day, and was fortunately for us acted upon as to many details of our Services, which a narrow and suspicious Puritanism would

Preface. xiii

have denied us. Is there less need for urging this generous large-hearted policy in our own day? Is it not manifest now, after a long, painful struggle, that it would have been far more for the peace of the Church, and the support of the principle of authority, if the vestment controversy had been settled rather by a wise and tolerant guidance by our superiors in accepting the revived zeal for restoration of a higher and more symbolic beauty of the Divine Service, than by an independent movement from below, subject to all kinds of irregular ventures and individual varieties? And is not the restoration of the Church's ancient custom of Reservation of the Blessed Sacrament for the sick a case to which such experience may profitably be applied?

It may be questioned whether to press this subject on the mind of the Church is strictly loyal, considering what took place so recently in the Upper Houses of Convocation, both of Canterbury and York. But it is not at all clear what was intended by the issuing of that Report, or how far it was meant to be considered as settling the question. It was said at the time by one of our leading and most learned bishops, the Bishop of Winchester, that to carry the Blessed Sacrament immediately out of the Church to the chamber of the sick was not to be counted as Reservation, yet that would be a step beyond what many had thought possible, besides implying that the Divine Presence remains permanently with the Consecrated Elements. And more recently, at the Canterbury Diocesan Conference, when that Resolution of the Upper House was referred to, his Grace the Primate made the significant remark that it was to be regarded as proceeding, not from Convocation itself, but from a Committee of that body. It may then be inferred that the subject, thus placed before the Church, is open to further consideration.

It is under these circumstances and with these convictions that I venture to plead for earnest attention to these pages. Whatever conclusions may be drawn from the facts and arguments adduced, it will be admitted by all that this important subject is dealt with in no controversial spirit, in perfect loyalty to the Church of England, with a simple desire for the truth and the best interests of the souls of men; and after a very careful and impartial study of all matters bearing on this traditional usage of the Church of Christ.

I may add that some may think that the title might have borne on its face a stronger affirmation of the claims advanced. It was thought best to keep the more modest line, rather than risk any appearance of a too positive assertion.

T. T. CARTER.

S. John's Lodge, Clewer,
Lent, 1887.

ERRATA.

Page 36, *for* "Galasius" *read* "Gelasius."

„ 75, note, *for* "Panormitanus" *read* "*Panormia* Ivonis."

„ 84, *for* "*consecratium*" *read* "*consecrantium.*"

„ 92, line 12, *for* "does not refer" *read* "does not of necessity refer."

„ 97, note, *for* "*aliquid, cadat*" *read* "*aliquid cadat.*"

„ 107, line 7, *read* "*Book of Common Prayer*, thus illustrated."

„ 146, line 10, *read* "so likewise with regard to Reservation;—while they enshrined, etc. . . . for the Communion of the sick and dying;—they gave no explicit direction," etc.

„ 152 and 153, note, *for* "Queens'" *read* "Queen's."

„ 160, line 3, *read* "communion rubric, in his commentary."

CHAPTER I.

INTRODUCTION.

THE primitive custom of reserving the Blessed Sacrament of the Eucharist for the communion of the sick and dying is here respectfully commended to the dispassionate consideration of the Bishops and Clergy of England, who, in virtue of their divine mission, canonical jurisdiction, and valid ordination, are the lawful custodians of Christ's holy mysteries in this land.

After a pastoral experience of more than twenty-five years in the priesthood, the author of this treatise begs very earnestly to submit to the Fathers of the Church and to his brethren of the Clergy that, under the present conditions of our social and ecclesiastical life, the spiritual needs of our people can only be satisfied by the restoration of this venerable usage which, notwithstanding its observance throughout the whole Church from the earliest times, has from a variety of causes fallen into disuse in England during the last three hundred years.

In advocating this restoration the writer desires to disclaim any intention of controversy; on the contrary he would rather suggest, in the interests of truth and charity, that this subject should be studied in the light of history, and would indicate to unprejudiced minds how much of primitive devotion underlies the familiar directions of the Book of Common Prayer; also that most providentially, as he ventures to think, the ancient Catholic order of reserving the Eucharist for the sick is still authorised by the Canon and Common Law of the Church of England.

This calm and judicial temper here desiderated is the more needed in an inquiry of this nature, because after so long a period, during which external intercommunion between ourselves and the rest of Catholic Christendom has been unhappily suspended, and in consequence the appeal of the Church of England to primitive antiquity has been but imperfectly realised, there is real danger lest in deciding a matter of Christian tradition, whether of faith or practice, men's minds should be biassed by insular, unhistoric, or even sectarian considerations. As a matter of fact English Christianity has drifted into a form of religionism which is in marked contrast with what we learn from history of that faith and worship which prevailed in the first ages of the Church, which of old expressed the devotion of our Catholic forefathers, and which in its leading characteristics has become traditional throughout the greater part of the Christian world. It is therefore not surprising that such a matter as the reservation of the holy Sacrament should be regarded with serious misapprehension, and that men should be slow to realise that this primitive custom is at once both significant and edifying as witnessing to the great principle of Christian unity that, whether communicating in church or detained by sickness at home, "we being many are one bread and one body, for we are all partakers of that one Bread."[1]

But though men have for the most part failed to realise that the faith and order of the Church must be traditional, and that whatever bears the *imprimatur* of primitive tradition is part of our heritage in the English Church, God has not been unmindful of that vine which He has planted in this land, and which He once made so strong for Himself.[2] Therefore the Holy Spirit of God, Who animates the One Body of Christ (the true Vine in Whom the several portions of the universal Church are incorporated as branches) is perpetually illuminating, informing, and guiding the faithful into the old paths, in order that the traditional system of the Church may be no mere abstract principle or archaic curiosity shut up in books and known only to a few, but a living, energising, and beneficent reality in the face of day.

[1] 1 Cor. x. 17. [2] Psalm lxxx.

Hence it has come to pass that, under the Divine guidance and by the supernatural power of the Holy Ghost, a great work of religious revival has been progressing during the last half century which has well nigh transformed the face of the Church in this land, and concerning which we are constrained to exclaim with reverence,—"This is the Lord's doing, and it is marvellous in our eyes."[1] All the complex organism of our ecclesiastical life has felt the touch of this wondrous power; men's minds have been recalled to the first principles of Christian faith, polity, and worship; the function of the Church as the extension of the Incarnation is again practically recognised, while the efficacy of the Sacraments as the *media* whereby living union with Christ, the "One Mediator between God and man,"[2] is initiated and sustained is again devoutly realised. Thus a great impulse has been given to the sacramental life of our people; in parishes where fifty or one hundred persons formerly communicated once a month, more than twice that number now communicate every week. Hence in manifold ways continually increasing demands are made upon the pastoral ministrations of the Clergy, particularly in spheres of missionary labour among the growing populations of our great towns.

As the result of this renewed life and appreciation of the holy Sacraments it is obvious that many

[1] Psalm cxviii. 23.   [2] 1 Tim. ii. 5.

Introduction. 5

problems need solution, which can only be dealt with in that spirit of "truth and peace"[1] which commends the observance of discipline in that temper of "moderation"[2] which mitigates the rigorous enforcement of the strict letter of the law.

Among these practical questions none surely calls more urgently for the spirit of equity in its consideration than that of reserving the Eucharist for the sick. The facts of daily experience make it abundantly evident that the needs of the sick and dying cannot be adequately supplied by rigidly insisting upon (what is assumed to be) the literal force of the later formularies of the Church of England, and therefore it is respectfully submitted that the spirit of the Church is most dutifully and intelligently observed by following the continuous stream of Catholic tradition in making provision for the communion of the sick and dying by reserving "the most comfortable Sacrament of the Body and Blood of Christ."[3]

It is hoped that in the following pages it will be made clear that this practice of reserving the Eucharist for the sick, which has hitherto been so imperfectly considered, is in harmony with Anglican formularies and implicitly sanctioned in the Book of Common Prayer; also that it may be regarded as

[1] Zech. viii. 16.   [2] Phil. iv. 5 (τὸ ἐπιεικὲς).
[3] Exhortation before Communion.

being still enjoined by the ancient and unrepealed Constitutions of the Province of Canterbury, which, as Bishop Gibson observes, having been received in the Province of York, are to this day embodied in the ecclesiastical laws of the English Church.[1]

[1] *Cf.* Bp. Gibson's *Codex Juris Ecclesiastici Anglicani*, Pref. x. xii. (London, 1713).

CHAPTER II.

RESERVATION OF THE EUCHARIST CONSISTENT WITH ANGLICAN FORMULARIES.

ATTENTION having been directed to the practice of reserving the Blessed Sacrament for the sick, by a Report of the Upper House of Convocation of the Province of Canterbury—a Report in which the Upper House of the Northern Province has since concurred—it is important that the formularies of the Church therein referred to should be rightly understood in their alleged reference to this custom.

They are as follows:—

1. The rubric at the close of the Communion Office.
2. The Order for the Communion of the Sick.
3. The Twenty-eighth Article of Religion.

At the outset it may frankly be admitted that, setting aside historical considerations, there is apparently in the above formularies considerable warrant for the conclusion arrived at. But it must be borne in mind that no documents of the Church can be rightly interpreted without taking fully into consideration the history of the circumstances under which they arose. The Bishops of England would not surely desire to adopt the policy of their brethren in the Vatican Council, by ignoring the fundamental principle of historical continuity as witnessing to the faith and practice of the Church of Christ.

What then is the force of the documents here referred to when viewed in the light of history?

1. The rubric at the close of the Communion Office first appears in the Liturgy which was drawn up (as is recorded) by Archbishop Laud and Bishop Wren for the Church of Scotland, and published in 1637. Previously there had been no such direction in the Book of Common Prayer; but at the revision of 1661 the Scotch rubric, as revised by Bishop Cosin, was adopted by Convocation and incorporated in our English Office.

In order adequately to estimate the scope and purport of this rubric, we must remember that the Prayer Book of 1559 contained no direction whatever respecting the consecrated Elements which might remain after the Communion, but simply ordered, at the end of the rubric concerning the sacramental bread, that "if any of the bread or wine remain, the Curate shall have it to his own use."

No doubt the old priests continued reverently to consume what remained as aforetime; but unhappily those of the Puritan faction brought in the innovation of using large pewter flagons holding two or three quarts apiece, such as may still be found in some old country churches, which after the Supper (as it was termed by them) were carried out of the church to their own tables! Accordingly, we find that Cosin, when Archdeacon of the East Riding, in his Visitation Articles of 1627, enquires:—

"Doth [your Parson, Vicar, or Curate] carefully see to the preparation of the bread and wine before every Communion, that they be pure and wholesome, that they be decently presented and placed upon the Table, that the quantitie thereof may be answerable to the number of his communicants, and that he prepareth or blesseth not twice as much as shall suffice, either to have it home to his house, or to tarry behind in the church, there with other people, in profane and common manner, to eate and to drinke at the Lord's Table and in the House of God?"[1]

Here then, in the profanation which Cosin and the orthodox clergy strove to check and in their efforts to promote reverence, which took shape in the Scottish Liturgy of 1637 and subsequently in the English Office of 1661, we find the origin of our present rubric.

It is therefore obvious that, so far from the rubric in question containing an absolute and unqualified "prohibition to take the consecrated remnants out of the church,"[2] as has been erroneously supposed, there was then no question of forbidding the primitive practice, at that time permitted, of

[1] *Bishop Cosin's Correspondence*, vol. i. p. 118 (Surtees Society, 1868).

[2] *Cf.* Correspondence in *The Guardian* upon *Reservation of the Sacrament* and *The Scottish Communion Office*, Mar. 4 and 11, 1885.

carrying the Eucharist to the sick. On the contrary, as we learn from contemporary history, the object of those in authority was to check the notorious scandals arising from the contempt of the Blessed Sacrament.

Hence the terms of the rubric of 1637 :—

"And if any of the bread and wine remain which is consecrated, it shall be reverently eaten and drunk by such of the communicants only as the presbyter which celebrates shall take unto him, but it shall not be carried out of the church."

And in order the more effectually to prevent the recurrence of abuses which had then only been too common, it is added :—

"And to the end there may be little left, he that officiates is required to consecrate with the least, and then if there be want, the words of consecration may be repeated again over more, either bread or wine."[1]

Thus it will be seen that our present rubric, which is substantially identical with the original as revised by Cosin, is directed against such profanation of the Sacrament as is specified in his Visitation Articles of 1627; and consequently that we are barred by its history from regarding it as prohibiting the primitive and Catholic custom of carrying the Holy Sacrament to the sick, and thereby contradicting the statement of the revisers themselves (in the preface to the Book of Common Prayer) to the effect that all such alterations were rejected "as were of dangerous consequence as

[1] *The Scottish Liturgy* (Edinburgh, 1637).

secretly striking at some established doctrine or laudable practice of the Church of England, or indeed of the whole Catholic Church of Christ."

Further evidence is likewise afforded respecting the intention of the rubric by Cosin himself in his *Considerations* (c. 1640) upon the Book of Common Prayer. In commenting on the rubric as it then stood, he observes:—

"It is likewise here ordered, 'That if any of the bread and wine remain, the curate shall have it to his own use.' Which words some curates have abused and extended so far, that they suppose they may take all that remains of the consecrated bread and wine itself home to their houses, and there eat and drink the same with their other common meats; at least the Roman Catholics take occasion hereby to lay this negligence and calumny upon the Church of England; whereas the rubric only intends it of such bread and wine as remain unconsecrate of that which was provided by the parish, (as appeareth by the articles of inquiry hereabouts in the visitations of divers bishops)."[1]

And once more, in order to emphasize our contention that in all the references to carrying the Sacrament out of church, the writers were invariably contemplating a profane carrying out of church, we adduce the following from a series of Notes, attributed to Bishop Overall, in an interleaved copy of the Prayer Book of 1619, which is preserved in Bishop Cosin's library at Durham:—

"*And if any of the bread and wine remain, etc.*—Which is not to be understood of the bread and wine already consecrated,

[1] *Cf.* Cosin's Works, vol. v. p. 519 (Library of Anglo-Catholic Theology, 1855).

but of that which remains without consecration; for else it were but a profanation of the holy Sacrament to let the curate have it home to his own use. *Quam indigne faciunt, qui hac rubrica ad tantum facinus excusandum abutuntur, ipsi viderint.*"[1]

2. With regard to the removal of all mention of reservation from the Order for the Communion of the Sick, it is to be noted that this is not due to our English Reformers, who distinctly made provision for such reservation, but to the influence of foreigners in 1552. There has, however, never been any prohibition of the ancient practice, as the Bishops would seem to imply; on the contrary, we learn from the Act of Uniformity authorising the second Prayer Book that no fault whatever was to be found with the first, which is characterised as "a very godly order . . . for Common Prayer and Administration of the Sacraments to be used in the mother tongue within the Church of England, agreeable to the

---

[1] The writer adds: "It was Nestorianism once to think that the consecrated bread, if it were kept *in crastinum*, became common bread again;" referring to S. Thomas Aquinas (*Summa Theologiæ*, pars. iii. quaest. 76, art. 6, ad secundum), who speaks of "quidam ponentes quod Corpus Christi non remaneat sub hoc sacramento, si in crastinum reservetur"; and quotes against them S. Cyril of Alexandria in his commentary on S. Luke xxii.: "Insaniunt quidam dicentes mysticam benedictionem cessare a sanctificatione, si quae ejus reliquiae remanserint in diem subsequentem; non enim mutatur sacratum Corpus Christi, sed virtus benedictionis et vivificativa gratia jugis in eo est." —*Ibid. cf.* pp. 130, 131.

These Notes of 1619 are undoubtedly in the handwriting of Cosin, and were certainly collected by him; though we may reasonably conclude that in so doing he adopted and transcribed the Notes entrusted to him by Bishop Overall and those of Bishop Andrewes.

Consistent with Anglican Formularies. 13

Word of God and the primitive Church." An order, moreover, which (ostensibly, at least) was merely altered "because," as the Act proceeds to state, "there hath arisen in the use and exercise of the aforesaid common service in the Church, heretofore set forth, divers doubts for the fashion and manner of the ministration of the same, rather by the curiosity of the minister and mistakers than of any other worthy cause."[1]

In fact, the rubric was simply dropped, as so many other important rubrics were dropped, in accordance with the policy then in vogue of conciliating the foreign Reformers; for instance, the rubrics enjoining the manual acts at the consecration of the Eucharist, which nevertheless undoubtedly continued to be observed. Thus Cosin himself tells us that although these directions were omitted in 1552, in consequence of Bucer's censure, "yet the use could not for all that be left off, it being a general custom among us to do so still."[2] Moreover, the rubric of the first Prayer Book directing reservation, though likewise omitted in 1552, was deliberately re-instated in the Latin Prayer Book of 1560, which was accepted by the clergy, and by them used concurrently with the English Book of 1559.

---

[1] 5 & 6 Edw. VI. c. 1.

[2] *Cf.* Cosin's *Notes upon the Common Prayer*. Third Series, p. 478; and *Considerations*, circ. 1640, p. 516.

A comparison of the Latin rubric with that of the first Prayer Book will shew that the celebration of the Eucharist in the sick chamber was provided for days on which there was no open communion in the church.[1]

Upon this question we have further the important testimony of Bishop Sparrow, himself one of the revisers in 1661. In his *Rationale upon the Book of Common Prayer* (first published in 1657, but of which the last edition in his lifetime was published in 1684, when the author was Bishop of Norwich) occurs the following passage:—

"The rubric at the communion of the sick directs the priest to deliver the communion to the sick, but does not set down how much of the Communion Service shall be used at the delivery of the communion to the sick; and therefore seems to me to refer us to former directions in times past."[2]

Whereupon the Bishop quotes at length the rubrics for the communion of the sick with the reserved Sacrament, and also when Holy Communion was celebrated in their presence, from the First Liturgy of King Edward VI. It is true that the rubric was amended in 1661; but even now, although it is perfectly clear what part of the office is to be used

[1] "Quod si contingat eodem die coenam Domini in ecclesia celebrari, tunc Sacerdos in coena tantum Sacramenti servabit quantum sufficit aegroto . . . . Sed si infirmus illo die petat communionem quo non celebratur coena, tunc Sacerdos in loco decenti, in domo aegroti celebrabit coenam."—*Cf. Communio Infirmorum.* (Liturgical Services of Queen Elizabeth, p. 404. Parker Society, Cambridge, 1847.)

[2] *Cf. Rationale* (London, 1684, re-edited with Preface by Card. Newman, Oxford, 1843), pp. 279—281. Also edition of 1722, pp. 223, 224.

when the priest celebrates the Holy Communion for the sick, no direction is given as to what course the priest is to adopt "if the same day (that the sick is to receive the Communion) there be a celebration of the Holy Communion in the church," in which case it would seem to be consistent with the present Order—as suggested by Bishop Sparrow— "to reserve at the open Communion so much of the Body and Blood as shall serve the sick person and so many as shall communicate with him." What also is to be done in case of the not infrequent possibility of finding "a convenient place in the sick man's house, with all things necessary so prepared that the curate may reverently minister"? In such cases (and they are by no means uncommon in the crowded dwellings of the poor and in many of our hospitals) are the sick to die without the *Viaticum* because of the supposed irregularity of carrying the Eucharist from the church? For it is to be observed that, apart from the conditions prescribed by the rubric,—namely, that there be "a convenient" that is, suitable "place in the sick man's house, with all things necessary so prepared," (*e.g.* bread and wine of the best and purest that may be had, sacred vessels of precious metal, and at least a surplice and a stole), "that the curate may reverently minister,"—the priest is not authorised by this Order for the Communion of the Sick in celebrating the divine Mysteries.

The rubrics for the communion of the sick with the reserved Sacrament are likewise cited (with evident approval) by Bishop Cosin in his *Notes upon the Book of Common Prayer*, without so much as a hint that in consequence of having been "omitted only and not condemned" (as he says elsewhere, see Chap. III. Sec. 2) they had either been forbidden or had ceased to be perfectly legitimate; adding significantly, "And of all this Order (even as it was in the second year of King Edward) Bucer gave his censure, 'That it was altogether agreeable to the word of God.'"[1]

Unhappily, Bucer subsequently changed his mind, as we may infer from the omission of the rubrics directing reservation; for Cosin tells us that at the review of the Service Book in 1552 "all things were presently ordered and altered according to his mind and censure."[2] Hence we are enabled, upon the great authority of Bishop Cosin, to account for this omission in our present Order, which we may hope the Bishops of the Church will eventually find the opportunity of repairing, by following the conspicuous example of fidelity to primitive custom afforded (in this respect) by our English Reformers in 1549.

Thus, upon due consideration of the peculiar

---

[1] Cosin's Works, vol. v. *Notes upon the Common Prayer.* Third Series, p. 497.
[2] *Ibid.* p. 479.

circumstances which prompted the omission of the rubric directing reservation, *viz.* the intemperance of foreign Zwinglians in the first instance, and subsequently the antipathy of English Puritans, we may surely conclude that, however needful it might be under such circumstances to abstain therefrom for a time, the mind of the Church has never been other than favourable to the retention of the primitive usage. Hence, apart from all direct injunctions, it would seem to be only a loyal adherence to the continuous tradition of the Church to re-introduce the practice whenever a suitable opportunity of doing so may occur.

Therefore, while valuing highly the privilege conceded in our present Order (in accordance with ancient precedent) of the private celebration for the communion of the sick,[1] it is nevertheless respect-

[1] In the ancient Service Books an Office was provided for celebration for the sick, and also for one at the point of death. Ven. Bede tells us that when S. Cuthbert lay dying the Eucharist was celebrated in his cell. ". . . . ecce sacer residens Antistes ad altar Pocula degustat vitae, Christique supinum Sanguine munit iter . . . ." Lo, the holy Bishop reclining before the altar tastes the Cup of Life, and with the Blood of Christ (defended) makes his heavenward way. *Cf. Vita S. Cudbercti Heroico Metro descripta.* Cap. xxxvi. Baedae *Hist. Eccles.*, etc., p. 286 (Cantab. 1722). Again, "Exitum suum . . . . Dominici corporis et sanguinis communione munivit." *Ibid.* p. 259. Bede's prose life of S. Cuthbert, Cap. 39. It would also appear from the Celtic Liturgical Remains, *e.g.* in the Irish fragments preserved at Trinity College, Dublin, in which we find a *Missa de Infirmis*, with Collects, Epistle, and Gospel, as in the present English Order for the Communion of the Sick; and from the *Ordo ad Communicandum Infirmum* in the Stowe Missal, which concludes with a Collect of

fully submitted to the generous consideration of our Fathers in God that the Catholic tradition of reserving the Eucharist in the church can alone provide for the exigencies of the sick and dying, and effectually meet the practical difficulties which continually arise in our crowded populations, and which otherwise must materially impede the usefulness of the clergy in their pastoral ministrations. Christ, we are told, had compassion on the multitude, because they had nothing to eat;[1] shall not the pastors of His flock be moved with a like compassion in supplying His famishing people with the spiritual food and sustenance which the good Shepherd has bequeathed to us in His holy Sacrament?

3. Respecting the declaration in the Twenty-eighth Article, it is fitting that we should be reminded of the explanation given by a bishop, himself one of the most accomplished theologians of modern times.

"The Article," says the late Bishop Forbes of Brechin, "does not prohibit the practices mentioned, but merely states

---

Thanksgiving for the Celebration of these holy Mysteries—*Deus, tibi gratias agimus per quem mysteria sancta celebravimus*—that, during the Celtic period of the Church in these islands, provision was made for celebrating the Eucharist in the sick man's house; while at the same time there is evidence that the consecrated Elements were reserved for those who were debarred by sickness or other urgent cause from communicating in church. *Cf. The Liturgy and Ritual of the Celtic Church*, by Rev. F. E. Warren, B.D., Fellow of S. John's Coll. Oxon. pp. 138, 164, 167, 220—225 (Oxford, 1881).

[1] S. Mark viii. 2.

that the reservation, circumgestation, elevation, and adoration of the *Sanctissimum* is no part of Christ's institution .... That the Sacrament of 'the Eucharist,' as the Latin articles term it, was not by Christ's ordinance reserved is admitted on all hands. The Council of Trent asserts that 'it was instituted that it might be received,' but the Church has from the earliest times reserved the Holy Sacrament, regarding it as a most precious pledge from heaven and the miracle of divine love. S. Justin Martyr says, that after celebration the Eucharistic elements were sent by the hands of the deacons to those not present. A touching instance of this is recorded in the act of the martyrdom of S. Lucian. In the second century it was the custom for Bishops to send It as a token of peace and unity. (*Epistle of Irenæus to S. Victor*, cited by Eusebius, *Hist. Eccles.* v. c. 24). That the Eucharist was reserved in the Church under both kinds from the fourth century is proved by S. Chrysostom in his letter to Pope Innocent, where the Saint describes the outrages of the soldiers in the Church of Constantinople .... Anciently the Sacrament was reserved .... for the communion of infants and of the sick, and for the *Missa Præsanctificatorum* both in the Roman, Greek, and Milanese Churches. In fact, till the thirteenth century, we have distinct evidence that in different ways, sometimes in a ciborium, sometimes suspended over the altar enveloped in veils, sometimes in tabernacles in the form of a dove, sometimes in aumbries beside the altar, sometimes along with images and relics of the saints, sometimes under baldachins, and sometimes in towers a few feet from the high altar, the Blessed Sacrament was reserved with great dignity and honour. The practice of reserving the Blessed Sacrament for the sick has obtained in the Scottish Church, by an unwritten tradition, since the days of the Non-jurors."[1]

It is most important to remember that Art. 28 was revised by the very men who replaced the rubric directing reservation in the Latin Prayer

---

[1] *Explanation of the Thirty-nine Articles*, by Bp. Forbes, pp. 566—569.

Book of 1560; clergy, be it observed, who, while yielding to the clamour of Zwinglianism by leaving in the article an obvious truism, nevertheless took the precaution at the same time to restore the rubric omitted in 1552, in testimony of their recognition of the mind of the Holy Ghost declared by the uniform practice of the Catholic Church.

These considerations dispose at once of the somewhat astonishing suggestion that this Article should be "read in connection with the direction" issued one hundred years later, under an entirely different state of things, and referring to a totally different subject. The rubric in connection with which the clause in the Article should be read is clearly that which was promulgated at the same time, and which, as a matter of fact, provides for that very reservation of "the Sacrament of the Eucharist" which this Article is assumed to forbid.

Thus we claim to have established this point:— That the reservation of the Sacrament for the sick is in nowise inconsistent with the rule of the Church of England.

CHAPTER III.

RESERVATION OF THE EUCHARIST RECOGNISED IN THE BOOK OF COMMON PRAYER.

1. The Ornaments rubric enjoins that the *Instrumenta* appertaining to Divine Service "shall be retained and be in use as were in this Church of England, by the authority of Parliament, in the second year of the reign of King Edward the Sixth."

Here it is important for us to remember that the second year of Edward VI. is precisely the last year (with the exception of the reign of Queen Mary) in which the Latin ritual was in use in the Church of England by the authority of Parliament. Up to this point there can be no doubt that the *Instrumenta* required for the safe custody of the Blessed Sacrament, then reserved in the church, and also for the carrying of the same to the sick with becoming honour, still continued to be in use, and therefore are enjoined still.

There is, however, a more restricted view of the Ornaments rubric, which limits its application to such Ornaments as were in use under the first

English Book of Common Prayer, authorised by Parliament in the Act of Uniformity passed Jan. 22, 1549, just within eight days of the close of the second year of the reign of King Edward VI.

But whichever hypothesis we adopt, the result is the same. For in that English Service Book of 1549 the practice of reservation for the sick, which heretofore had been customary in accordance with the Canon and Common Law of the Church, was now enjoined in her Offices. This direction therefore, in virtue of the authority of Parliament, now acquired the force of Statute Law.

Moreover, when we remember the conservative character of the English Reformation, it is but reasonable to conclude that the Sacrament of the Eucharist would still be carried to the sick with becoming reverence as aforetime.

For instance, the "two lights upon the high altar before the Sacrament," which had formerly been used in time of Mass, as ordained in the Provincial Constitutions,[1] were again enjoined in the Injunctions of Edward VI. "for the signification that Christ is the very true light of the world."

---

[1] The Constitution of Abp. Walter, A.D. 1322, directing that in time of Mass two candles shall be lighted, or at least one—*Tempore quo Missarum Solemnia peraguntur, accendantur duae candelae, vel ad minus una.* Upon which Lyndwood observes, in words which have evidently suggested the reason stated in the Injunction of Edward VI., *Candela namque sic ardens significat Ipsum Christum, qui est splendor Lucis aeternae.* Cf. Bp. Gibson's *Codex*, I. 471 (London, 1713); and Lyndwood's *Provinciale*, 236 (Oxon. 1679).

No doubt, therefore, the light required by the Constitution of Archbishop Peccham, with the bell to give warning to the faithful, and the decent Pyx[1] for the seemly carrying of the Eucharist, would continue to be in use whensoever the King of Glory, veiled in His holy Sacrament, might visit His suffering people, to sustain and gladden them in the most holy Communion of His blessed Body and Blood.

2. The next step in our argument arises from the consideration that that part of the preface in the Book of Common Prayer, entitled, *Of Ceremonies, why some be abolished and some retained*, was originally prefixed to the Service Book of 1549, and has been retained without alteration in all subsequent revisions. Upon this point we cannot do better than quote at length the weighty testimony of Bishop Cosin to the importance of this fact:—

"This preface is the same verbatim with that which is in the Service Book of King Edward VI. (*i.e.* of 1549). The preface then being retained, it seems all the ceremonies of that book are still justified by our Church, though some of them, at Calvin's and Bucer's instance, were omitted in the review of the book 5 Edw. VI. as not accounted absolutely necessary."[2]

" Of such ceremonies as be used in the Church,"

[1] In the Register of Walter Gray, Archbishop of York, A.D. 1250, we find the Pyx—*Pyxis pro corpore Christi honesta*—included among the Church Ornaments to be provided by the parishioners. *Cf. The York Pontifical*, p. 372 (Surtees Society, 1873).

[2] *Cf.* Library of Anglo-Catholic Theology. Cosin's Works, vol. v. *Notes on the Book of Common Prayer*, 1st Series, p. 12.

says the Preface, "and have had their beginning by the institution of man, some of the first were of godly intent and purpose devised, and yet at length turned to vanity and superstition."

Upon this statement Cosin, probably following Bishop Overall, thus comments:—

"None of these can be meant of any ceremonies used in King Edward's first Service Book, for that book has these very words, and therefore they must be meant of other ceremonies, which they in the Church of England at that time refused, and of none other that are since omitted. I say omitted only, and not condemned; for if our Church had meant to condemn the ceremonies used in that book, they would never have taken the same discourse about ceremonies to do it, which is here used to approve and authorise them; but they would have made some other of set purpose to condemn them."[1]

Again, in meeting the unreasonable cavil of those persons who are offended "for that some of the old ceremonies are retained still," the writer, adopting Hooker's argument, continues:—

"Those which make so perilous a matter of our retaining those ceremonies, common to us as with the Church of Rome, do seem to imagine that we have of late erected a frame of some new religion . . . . whereas in truth we have continued the old religion; and the ceremonies which we have taken from them that were before us are not things that belong to this or that sect, but they are the ancient rites and customs of the Church of Christ, whereof ourselves being a part we have the self-same interest in them which our fathers before us had, from whom the same descended unto us."[2]

Among these "ancient rites and customs of the

[1] Cosin's Works, *Notes on the Book of Common Prayer*, p. 12.
[2] *Ibid*, p. 13; also Hooker, *Eccles. Polity* [ed. 1622, Bk. iv. 9, § 1].

Church of Christ" is that of reserving the Eucharist for the needs of the sick and dying, and for those who in days of persecution or in case of other urgent necessity were debarred from communicating in church. It is evident, therefore, that inasmuch as the rite of Reservation for the Sick (with its accustomed ceremonial) was expressly retained in the Prayer Book of 1549, it cannot be included in the category of ceremonies which have been abolished, and consequently must still be regarded as being among those which are implicitly recognised in the Book of Common Prayer.

3. But the most important and direct recognition of the principle of reserving the Holy Sacrament is to be found in the Eucharistic Office itself.

The rubric which follows the distribution of Holy Communion directs, in terms indeed of great simplicity, but which clearly indicate a reverend estimation for Christ's holy Mysteries, that:—

"When all have communicated, the Minister[1] shall return to the Lord's Table, and reverently place upon it what remaineth of the consecrated Elements, covering the same with a fair linen cloth."

This beautiful and significant action is so familiar to us, and the history and liturgical force of this

---

[1] The more general designation "minister" is here used as applying to each of the officiating clergy; because, although the assistants would reverently place the sacred vessels upon the altar by the hands of the celebrant, it would be the duty of the deacon to assist the priest in this ministration, and reverently to veil the Blessed Sacrament.

rubric have been so little regarded, that its pregnant meaning has been generally unnoticed, as though the observance it enjoins were merely a matter of practical convenience. Whereas this rubric, when historically and liturgically examined, particularly when its bearing upon the dignified Post-Communion of the English rite is adequately considered, will be seen to be a precious link binding us to the earlier usage of the Western Church; while its dogmatic importance will be recognised as witnessing to the permanent sacredness of the consecrated Elements.

(i) The history of this rubric is full of interest and significance. It is attributed, in the first instance, to Archbishop Laud and his friend and fellow-labourer Bishop Wren, under whose auspices it was inserted in the Scotch Liturgy of 1637; in which we find it in the following terms:—

"When all have communicated, he that celebrates shall go to the Lord's Table and cover, with a fair linen cloth or corporal,[1] that which remaineth of the consecrated Elements."

---

[1] That is, the *corporalia calicis* of the Sarum rite, as distinct from the corporal upon which the Oblations were placed in the centre of the altar. Thus we find the following rubric in the Sarum Missal at the Oblation of the elements: *Dictaque Oratione, reponat calicem et cooperiat cum corporalibus, ponatque panem super corporalia decenter ante calicem vinum et aquam continentem.*

The corporal, as we learn from Durandus, was in some churches of an oblong form, extended lengthwise along the table of the altar; he tells us also that two corporals were used, the one which the deacon extended in the midst of the altar to receive the vessels and oblations, the other which was placed folded upon the chalice. This latter became

Under the Service Book of 1549, in which the ancient order of the Sarum Mass was for the most part retained, there can be little doubt that (in case the celebrant did not reserve for the sick) he would naturally receive what might remain of the consecrated elements, together with the Ablutions for the cleansing of the chalice and paten,[1] immediately

eventually represented by the *parva palla linea* of the Roman rite, which is now more conveniently used for the covering of the chalice. But it is clear from Durandus (as also from the Sarum rubric) that anciently a "corporal" was used for this purpose; *e.g.* he says (*inter alia*) "diaconus discooperit calicem inde removens corporale"; while in the *palla corporalis* (an expression used by Durandus as synonymous with *corporale*) we find the connecting link between the *corporalia calicis* of the Sarum rite and the *palla* of later times. *Cf. Rationale Divinorum Officiorum*, by Will. Durandus, formerly Bishop of Mende, lib. iv. cap. xxix. li. (Venice, 1540).

It is, however, to be noted that, according to the present Roman rite, when the Sacrament is reserved until the end of Mass (as on Maundy Thursday) an additional veil is to be used for covering the same; and in this veil probably we find the counterpart to the "fair linen cloth" prescribed for the like purpose in the English rite.

[1] "Si vero de Patina, sicut quidam faciunt, [Hostiam] sumat, post celebrationem Missae tam Patinam quam calicem faciat aqua perfundi." —(Const. Abp. Edmund, A.D. 1246). Hence we learn that the blessing of the bread upon the paten, as directed in the present English rite, and not upon the corporal, as in the Roman rite, is in accordance with early English precedent. Both these usages were recognised in the Liturgy of 1549, in which the rubric at the Offertory contains the direction—"*laying the bread upon the corporas, or else in the paten, or in some other comely thing prepared for that purpose,*" e.g. a *ciborium*, which may conveniently be used in case of a large number of communicants.

This Constitution of Archbishop Edmund is also interesting as indicating that it was the ancient practice in England to take the Ablutions *post celebrationem Missae*, and not immediately after the receiving of Holy Communion,—a precedent evidently followed in our after the administration of Holy Communion. But the transposition of the Prayer of Oblation and *Gloria in Excelsis* to the Post-Communion, in the subsequent editions of the Prayer Book, made it desirable that the Sacrament should be reserved until the end of the Office, as in the earlier ages of the Church. Whether this change was practically made, in the absence of any specific direction, may be an open question; certain it is that the Puritan clergy did reserve the Sacrament until the end of the service, though for profane and common uses.

We need not wonder, therefore, that the Caroline divines, learned as they undoubtedly were in the liturgical usages of Catholic antiquity, should have retained and enjoined the reservation of the Sacrament, while at the same time they carefully guarded against the profanation which, under Puritan misuse, had unhappily accompanied it.

That in so doing they proceeded advisedly is clear from Bishop Cosin's reference to Bucer's censures upon the Prayer Book of 1549; in which Cosin thus states Bucer's exception to the Offertory rubric, *Then shall the Minister take so much Bread and Wine as shall suffice for the persons appointed to receive the Holy Communion, etc.:—*

"That the minister should be enjoined to provide no more

present rite, in the rubric which directs the reverent consumption of what remains of the consecrated elements "immediately after the Blessing." *Cf.* Lyndwood, *Provinciale* (Oxon. 1679), pp. 234–5.

Recognised in the Prayer Book. 29

bread and wine upon the altar than would serve the people that communicate, he misliketh utterly; because by this injunction men would be brought to an opinion that what was left of the elements after the Communion was done may not be put to any common use; but that (as of old, in the ancient father's time, they were wont to do) whatever remaineth was to be taken and eaten by the communicants in the church. Which, because it was like to confirm the papists in their conceit that the nature of the bread and wine were changed, and that Christ was inherent in the elements themselves, he urged to have it declared that *extra usum Sacramenti*, that is, when the Communion was ended the bread and wine might be put to any common use."[1]

This passage is important on account of its historical bearing upon the rubric immediately before us, and also because of the additional light it throws upon the concluding rubric (already considered), which now specifically ordains that "if any remain of that which is consecrated, it shall not be carried out of the church"; or, in Cosin's words, "may not be put to any common use."

Moreover, it affords further evidence that this latter rubric was not intended to forbid reservation, concerning which no controversy then existed, but was deliberately adopted to guard against the profanation of Christ's holy Mysteries, and to ensure the reverent consumption of the consecrated elements; and that in this respect the revisers were proceeding in accordance with the "order taken of old for it in the Church, which (as Cosin, following

---

[1] *Cf.* Cosin's Works, vol. v. *Notes upon the Book of Common Prayer*, Third Series, p. 476.

Bishop Overall, says elsewhere) were well to be observed still."[1]

And "as of old, in the ancient fathers' time," the Catholic custom of reservation confessedly co-existed with the observance here referred to—that "whatever remained was to be taken and eaten by the communicants in the church"—it follows that reservation is still implicitly recognised in this present rubric, which, as we here learn from Bishop Cosin, was intended to restore the ancient practice of the Church.

Hence the historical consideration of this significant action in the English Liturgy clearly shews that in this Post-Communion rubric, taken in conjunction with that at the end of the Office, enjoining the reverent consumption of the consecrated Elements, we have a distinct reversal of the anti-sacramental policy adopted at the instance of Bucer and Calvin in 1552; and further, that both these rubrics are based upon the fundamental truth of Christ's objective presence in the Eucharist, or, in the forcible words of Bishop Cosin, who penned these rubrics, "that Christ was inherent in the Elements themselves," and that these directions are only intelligible upon this hypothesis.

The following evidence to the accuracy of this conclusion is most important, not only as having

---

[1] Cosin's Works, vol. v. *Notes upon the Book of Common Prayer*, First Series, p. 131.

been written by Cosin himself in commenting upon the final rubric before the provision for the reverent consumption of the consecrated Elements was inserted in 1661, but also as expressing the teaching of his "lord and master, Dr. Overall," who wrote the latter part of the Church Catechism concerning the Sacraments:—

"It is confessed by all divines that upon the words of consecration the Body and Blood of Christ is really and substantially present, and so exhibited and given to all that receive it; and all this not after a physical and sensual, but after a heavenly and invisible and incomprehensible, manner. But yet there remains this controversy among some of them, whether the Body of Christ be present only in the use of the Sacrament and in the act of eating, and not otherwise. They that hold the affirmative, as the Lutherans . . . . and all Calvinists do, seem to me to depart from all antiquity, which places the presence of Christ in the virtue of the words of consecration and benediction used by the priest, and not in the use of eating of the Sacrament, for they tell us that the virtue of that consecration is not lost, though the Sacrament be reserved either for sick persons or other."[1]

Hence it is plain that neither Bishop Overall nor Cosin were cognisant of any rubric or canon prohibiting the primitive and Catholic custom of reserving the Blessed Sacrament for the sick; and since, so far as we know, the question of forbidding it was not so much as raised at the last revision of the Book of Common Prayer in 1661, we cannot resist the conclusion that it continues to be perfectly legitimate.

[1] Cosin's Works, vol. v. *Notes upon the Book of Common Prayer*, First Series, p. 131.

(ii) By the liturgical consideration of this rubric is to be understood the evidences of its analogy to similar directions in other liturgies, and its conformity to the general tradition of the Church.

There is a remarkable counterpart to this rubric in the directions in the Roman Missal respecting the reservation of the Blessed Sacrament in the Mass of Maundy Thursday, a provision, be it observed, which, as we learn from the *Ritus Servandus* at the beginning of the missal, is contemplated at other times as occasion may require. By these directions the priest is enjoined to reserve the Sacrament for the Mass of the Pre-sanctified upon Good Friday, because upon that day there is no consecration; and also for the communion of the sick, and to place the reserved Host in another chalice, which the deacon covers with the paten and pall, and then, spreading a veil over the same, places it in the midst of the altar. Similar directions for reserving the Holy Sacrament on Maundy Thursday are prescribed in the English Uses of Sarum, Hereford, and York.

The origin of all such directions is to be found in the ancient customs of the Church. For instance, Amalarius, bishop of Trêves, writing early in the ninth century, witnesses to the observance of a liturgical usage analagous to that prescribed by our English rubric in the reservation of a portion of the Host until the end of Mass. The passage is so beautiful as to be worthy of being quoted in full. It is headed :—

"*De parte oblatæ, quæ remanet in altari*.[1]—Triforme est corpus Christi, eorum scilicet qui gustaverunt mortem et morituri sunt. Primum videlicet sanctum et immaculatum, quod assumptum ex Maria virgine : Alterum, quod ambulat in terra : Tertium, quod jacet in sepulchris. Per particulam oblatæ immissæ in calicem, ostenditur Christi corpus, quod jam resurrexit a mortuis. Per commestam a sacerdote vel a populo, ambulans adhuc super terram. Per relictam in altari usque ad finem Missæ, jacens in sepulchris usque ad finem sæculi . . . .

"Remanetque in altari ipsa particula usque ad finem Missæ : Quia usque in finem sæculi corpora sanctorum quiescent in sepulchris. Munditiam mentis docet corporale,[2] quod remanet in altari post domini resurrectionem, cui debet unus quisque semper studere accipiens corpus domini, sed præcipue in fine."

No commentary upon the present English rite could be more appropriate and beautiful than these words of the age of Alfred the Great and Charlemagne.

Evidence to the same effect is to be found in the ancient anonymous treatise entitled, *Gemma animæ* —*De antiquo ritu Missarum*.[3]

Also in Micrologus, *De Missa rite celebranda* (written probably *circ.* A.D. 800), who explains the custom of reserving the remaining portion of the Sacrament in similar words :—

---

[1] *Speculum Missæ*, à Joanne Cochleo (Venetiis, 1572). *Cf.* Amalarius, *De Officio Missæ*, cap. xxxv. p. 44.

[2] *Corporale*,—evidently the "fair linen cloth" used in veiling the reserved Sacrament, and so named in the Scotch Liturgy of 1637.

[3] *Ibid. De tribus partibus oblatæ*, cap. lvi. p. 132 *b*.

"Tertium quod jam requiescit in Christo, quod etiam in tertiâ particulâ in altari reservatâ apte figuratur, quam viaticum morientium apellare solemus." [1]

From Durandus, the famous liturgist of medieval times, we learn that the custom of reserving the consecrated Elements until the end of Mass was certainly observed in the Roman Church, most probably in all the Churches of the West, if not indeed throughout the whole Christian world, in the time of Pope Gelasius, in the fifth century. His words are:—

"Secundum Gelasium Papam, pars in calice posita significat Corpus Christi quod de virgine traxit; pars sicca comesta significat omnes fideles; pars reservata usque in finem missae, secundum antiquum ecclesiæ Romanæ morem, pro ministris vel infirmis, significat omnes mortuos." [2]

The explanation of the same custom by Pope Sergius, likewise recorded by Durandus, is almost identical with that which has already been cited from Amalarius. This usage is also referred to by Card. Bona, as being formerly enjoined in the *Ordo Romanus*.

"Olim fractâ hostiâ, una pars servabatur usque ad finem Missæ . . . Ordo quoque Romanus ait, particulam oblatæ quam frangit Pontifex, ab eo relinqui super altare." [3]

---

[1] *Ibid. cf.* cap. xvii. *Corpus Christi tripliciter consideratur*, p. 144 b.

[2] *Cf. Rationale Divinorum Officiorum* . . . editum per reverendum dominum Gulielmum Durantum, quondam Episcopum Mimaten. (Venetiis, MDXXXX), lib. iv. cap. li.

[3] *Cf. Joannis Bonæ Opera, Rerum Liturgicarum*, lib. II. cap. xv. 4 (Antverpiæ, 1677).

Thus we learn from Pope Gelasius and others that the familiar custom of reserving the remaining part of the consecrated Elements until the end of Mass, now enjoined in our English rubric, was regarded as an ancient custom in the Roman Church in the fifth century. We may, therefore, infer that it was observed in the pontificate of S. Sylvester, who, in the previous century, under Constantine the Great, regulated the then existing traditions of that church; and consequently that it may be reckoned among those liturgical usages which are derived from the holy Apostles themselves.

It is likewise worthy of note that the final rubric which provides for the reverent consumption of what is thus reserved, and which, as we have seen from Bishop Cosin, was intended to restore the ancient order of the Church, is entirely in harmony with the ancient custom referred to by Pope Gelasius, from whom we learn that the reserved Sacrament was received by the ministers or by the sick. And so we have additional evidence that, while the Post-Communion rubric distinctly enjoins the liturgical usage of reservation anciently observed, the provisions of the final rubric are perfectly consistent with the primitive custom of reserving the Blessed Sacrament for the sick; and that, in the light of primitive antiquity, its restrictive force (intended to guard against profanation) is seen to have no further reference to the custom of reservation than in directing that what is not so required for the sick shall be reverently consumed.

In this reference to the liturgical practice of reservation there is no specific mention of the chalice; we cannot, however, but reasonably infer, from the well-known teaching of S. Galasius[1] respecting the necessity of the communion of the chalice to the completeness of the Eucharistic Mystery, that in his time the consecrated Elements under both kinds were reserved until the end of Mass, and that what was not required for the communion of the sick was then reverently consumed by the priest and his ministers.

And therefore the liturgical consideration of this rubric leads to the conclusion that in the present English rite we have a remarkable counterpart to the traditional usage of the primitive Church.

(iii) One important point, however, remains still to be considered, namely, the relation of the Holy Sacrament thus reverently reserved upon the altar to the Post-Communion prayers of our English rite.

It is well known that Bishop Cosin endeavoured

---

[1] The following passage from Micrologus, citing the teaching of S. Gelasius respecting the obligation of communion in both kinds, is too important to be omitted. "Beatus Gelasius Papa, ... scribens quibusdam Episcopis, excommunicari illos præcepit, quicumque, sumpto corpore dominico, a calicis participatione abstinerent. Nam (ut ipse in eodem decreto asserit) hujusmodi Sacramentorum divisio, sine grandi sacrilegio provenire non poterit."—Micrologus *de Missa rite celebranda*, circ. 800. *Cf. Speculum Missæ* (Venetiis, MDLXXII.) 145 *b*.

at the last revision of the Book of Common Prayer to restore the Prayer of Oblation to its old position immediately after the Consecration, from which it had been transposed to the Post-Communion in the revision of 1552. In this effort he was unsuccessful, and students of the Prayer Book are familiar with the significant note in Sancroft's hand :—"*My Lords the Bishops at Ely House ordered all in the old method.*"

But though Cosin failed in effecting the return to the ancient order which he desired, he did secure the adoption of this rubric which we have been considering, and which has proved effectual not only in bringing our English rite into harmony with ancient usage with respect to the reservation and consumption of the consecrated Elements, but in rectifying the displacement of 1552 by virtually providing that the Prayer of Oblation shall be said *coram sacramento*, while the *Gloria in Excelsis* thus becomes a noble act of Eucharistic worship.

The liturgical importance of this prayer in its relation to the Holy Sacrament is obvious to all who are conversant with the teaching of Holy Scripture, and the witness of the primitive liturgies, concerning that elementary principle of mediation which underlies the Eucharistic mystery.

This is set forth at length in Cosin's valuable exposition of the Eucharistic Sacrifice in his *Notes upon the Book of Common Prayer*.

From these *Notes* we cite the following :—

"*O Lord and heavenly Father.*] In King Edward's first Service Book this prayer was set before the delivery of the Sacrament to the people, and followed immediately after the consecration; and certainly it was the better and the more natural order of the two; neither do I know whether it were the printer's negligence, or no, thus to displace it. For the consecration of the Sacrament being ever the first, it was always the use in all liturgies to have the oblation follow (which is this), and then the participation, which goes before, and after all the thanksgiving, which is here set next before the *Gloria in Excelsis*; in regard whereof I have always observed my lord and master Dr. Overall to use this oblation in its right place, when he had consecrated the Sacrament to make an offering of it (as being the true public sacrifice of the Church) unto God, that by the merits of Christ's death, which was now commemorated, all the Church of God might receive mercy, etc., as in this prayer; and when that was done he did communicate the people, and so end with the thanksgiving following hereafter. If men would consider the nature of this Sacrament, how it is the Christian sacrifice also, they could not choose but use it so too; for as it stands here it is out of its place. We ought first to send up Christ unto God, and then He will send Him down unto us."[1]

If this prayer were said after the consumption of the consecrated Elements it would obviously be deprived of its liturgical significance, but being now said (in virtue of this rubric) in presence of the reserved Sacrament, no words can express its moving power in pleading the merits of Christ's death and passion on behalf of the whole Church of God. This oblation of the most precious Body and Blood of Christ, veiled upon the altar, thus evidently

---

[1] Cosin's Works, vol. v. *Notes upon the Book of Common Prayer,* First Series, p. 114.

becomes our *Sacrificium Laudis*, honouring God; our *Sacrificium Eucharisticum*, thanking Him; our *Sacrificium Propitiatorium*, rendering Him favourable to us; and our *Sacrificium Impetratorium*, supplicating His grace and mercy on behalf of all for whom we are bound to pray.

In the words of Bishop Cosin, commenting upon this prayer,—*That by the merits and death of Thy Son Jesus Christ, and through faith in His Blood, we and all Thy whole Church, etc.*:—

"This is a plain oblation of Christ's death once offered, and a representative sacrifice of it, for the sins, and for the benefit of the whole world, of the whole Church; that both those which are here on earth, and those that rest in the sleep of peace, being departed in the faith of Christ, may find the effect and virtue of it. And if the authority of the ancient Church may prevail with us, as it ought to do, there is nothing more manifest than that it always taught as much. And it is no absurdity to say, here is an oblation made for all, when it is not only commemorated to have been once offered, but solemn prayers are here also added, and request made that it may be effectual for all.—S. Chrys. *in Matt. viii.*

"And in this sense it is not only an eucharistical but a propitiatory sacrifice. [And to prove it a sacrifice propitiatory, always so acknowledged by the ancient Church, there can be no better argument than that it was offered up, not only for the living but for the dead, and for those that were absent, for them that travelled, for Jews, for heretics, etc., who could have no other benefit of it, but as it was a propitiatory sacrifice; and that thus they did offer it, read a whole army of fathers, *apud* Mald. *de Sacr.* p. 342, etc., *Nos autem ita comparati sumus, ut cum tam multis et magnis authoribus errare malimus, quam cum Puritanis verum dicere.*] Not that it makes any propitiation, as that of the cross did, but that it obtains and brings into act that propitiation which was once made by Christ; and so we may speak of prayer, for that is propitiatory too.¹

"Why should we then make any controversy about this? They love not the truth of Christ, nor the peace of the Church, that make these disputes between the Church of Rome and us, when we agree, as Christian Churches should, in our Liturgies: what private men's conceits are, what is that to the public approved religion of either Church, which is to be seen in their Liturgies best of all? For let the schools have what opinions and doctrines they will, and let our new masters frame themselves what divinity they list, as long as neither the one nor the other can get their fancies brought into the service of the Church, honest men may serve God with one heart and one soul, and never trouble themselves with the opinions of them both."²

We need offer no apology in thus citing the important testimony of the leading reviser in 1661 to the sacrificial intention of the Prayer of Oblation, which emphasises the significance of the previous rubric, now providing that this prayer, though still placed in the Post-Communion, shall be said in the presence of Christ's holy Mysteries,—a provision, be it observed, which invests the whole of the Post-Communion with a sacramental character, and thus accentuates the sacrificial nature of this sacred action.

Thus in commenting upon the following clause,—

---

[1] "Atque hac ratione hoc sacrificium, quatenus sacerdotis pia supplicatione peragitur, non modo eucharisticum, sed etiam propitiatorium dici possit, non quidem ut efficiens propitiationem, quod sacrificio crucis proprium est, sed ut eam jam factam impetrans, quomodo oratio, cujus hoc sacrificium species est, propitiatoria dici potest."—Cassander's *Consultatio*. *Cf.* Cosin's Works, vol. v. pp. 119, 120.

[2] *Ibid.* p. 120.

And here we offer and present unto Thee, O Lord, ourselves, our souls and bodies, to be a reasonable, holy, and lively sacrifice unto Thee,—Cosin, adopting the words of S. Augustine, adds:—

"*Christus est sacerdos, Ipse offerens, et Ipse oblatio. Cujus rei Sacramentum quotidianum esse voluit Ecclesiæ sacrificium, quæ cum Ipsius capitis corpus sit, seipsam per Ipsum discit offerre.* S. Aug. *de Civitate Dei*, lib. x. cap. 20.[1]

Bishop Sparrow, the learned author of the *Rationale,* also witnesses to the special fitness of the *Gloria in Excelsis* as an act of Eucharistic worship.

"Then we say or sing the angelic hymn, *Glory be to God on high, etc.*, wherein the ecclesiastical hierarchy does admirably imitate the heavenly, singing this at the Sacrament of His body which the angels did at the birth of His body. And good reason there is to sing this for Christ's being made one with us in the Sacrament, as for His being made one of us at His birth. And if ever we be fit to sing this angels' song it is when we draw nearest to the estate of angels, namely, at the receiving of the Sacrament."[2]

It is true that these words were originally written before the rubric directing the liturgical reservation of the Sacrament was inserted at the last revision; they may not therefore, in the first instance, have referred to the continued presence of the Eucharist upon the altar, though there is ground for concluding that this usage (enjoined in the Scotch Liturgy of 1637) had become traditional in

---

[1] Cosin's Works, vol. v. p. 352; *cf.* p. 120.

[2] *Rationale upon the Common Prayer* (London, 1684, re-edited by Card. Newman, Oxford, 1843), p. 226. Also edition of 1722, p. 181.

England subsequently to 1559; but inasmuch as the reference to singing the *Gloria in Excelsis* "at the Sacrament of His body" clearly recognises the Lord's body as an objective reality external to ourselves, as to the angels who sang their praises at His birth (and the *Rationale* was repeatedly re-edited by its venerable author after the revision of 1661), we may reasonably infer that the words in question do reverently contemplate the Lord's presence in the Sacrament, and also His no less real presence with His faithful people "who have duly received these holy Mysteries."

Finally, the solemn Blessing at the conclusion of the Liturgy acquires special significance in consequence of this rubric, which virtually directs that it shall be given in presence of the Eucharist.

We learn from Durandus, and from the ancient liturgical uses of the Western Church, that the Blessing followed the fraction of the Host, when the priest placed a particle thereof in the chalice, in token of Christ's resurrection, in which His body and soul were reunited after being sundered in sacrificial death, saying, *Pax Domini sit semper vobiscum.* The remaining portions having been placed upon the paten, to be in readiness for the priest's communion and for that of the people, or for the communion of any sick persons for whom they might be reserved, the celebrant turned towards the people from the gospel side of the altar, and in presence of the Blessed Sacrament gave the solemn Benediction. We learn further from Cardinal Bona that, except in the Mozarabic rite, this solemn Benediction, as distinguished from the Blessing at the end of Mass in the later Roman rite, was given exclusively by the bishop;[1] and it was thus given immediately after the mystical symbol of the resurrection and in presence of the Eucharist, to signify the Blessing given by the risen Christ, when He stood in the midst of His assembled Church and said, "Peace be unto you." Micrologus tells us that originally there was no Blessing at the end of Mass, for the following reason:—

"Nam soli communicantes confectioni Sacramentorum antiquitus intererant, quibus et oratio post Communionem, quæ pro solis communicantibus instituta est, pro benedictione potuit satisfacere. Apud modernos [*i.e.* circ. A.D. 800] autem, cum jam populus communicare cessaret, nec tamen divinis mysteriis se subtraheret, necessario permissum est, ut a presbytero benediceretur, ne tam benedictione quam communione privatus discedere videretur."[2]

This *Benedictio post Missam*, so far as is apparent from the uses of Sarum, York, and Hereford, was never part of the ancient usage of the Church of England. But there is reason to believe that as priests were enjoined, according to the Mozarabic rite, to give the solemn Benediction in the absence

[1] *Cf.* Bona, *Rerum Liturgicarum*, lib. II. xvi.
[2] *Cf.* Micrologus, *de Missa rite celebranda, Speculum Missæ*, (*Venetiis*, MDLXXII.) p. 147.

of the bishop, so likewise, under the ancient Gallican and English uses, the same custom originally prevailed.[1] This opinion is strengthened by the letter of S. Jerome to the Bishop of Narbonne, cited by Micrologus, "who asserts that priests are not to be debarred from giving the liturgical Blessing. If," he asks, "a priest is empowered to consecrate the body of Christ in the blessing of the sacramental Elements at the altar of God, is it not likewise his duty to bless the people of God?" And then he gives to the bishop the following counsel: "That in the churches of his diocese his presbyters should follow the custom observed in Rome, in the East, in Africa, in Spain, in Britain, and in Gaul, and in all places where humility prevails."[2]

[1] Mabillon, cited by Maskell, *Ancient Liturgy of the Church of England*, second edition (London, 1846), p. 110, says that the same provision was made very anciently in the Gallic Liturgy. *De Lit. Gall.* lib. i. 4, 13.

[2] Micrologus, *ut supra*, p. 146 *b*. *Cf.* Bona, *Rerum Liturgicarum*, lib. ii. cap. xvi., where reference is made to the ancient Gallican Missal and likewise to Canon 28 of the first Council of Orleans, which directs that, "When the people are come together in the Name of God to the celebration of Mass, let them not depart until the solemnity of Mass is ended; and, if the bishop be not present, let them receive the Blessing from the priest," the Blessing here referred to being the Benediction (ordinarily given by the bishop after the Lord's Prayer), for there was then no Blessing at the end of Mass. It is true that according to the ancient liturgical uses of England, as they have come down to us from medieval times, the Episcopal Benediction was given after the fraction of the Host and *before* the particle thereof was placed in the chalice; but it is not unlikely that, in consequence of the absence of rubrical directions in the earlier missals, the later custom may have deviated from that of former ages. For instance, the 17th Canon of the fourth

In the English Liturgy of 1549 the priest was directed to dismiss the people with the Blessing at the end of Mass, as in the present Roman rite; whereas in 1661, in virtue of the rubrics then inserted, providing for the reservation of the consecrated Elements and their subsequent consumption "after the Blessing," a distinct return was made to the earlier usage of the Church. Consequently the solemn liturgical Blessing is now given by the bishop, or in his absence by the priest, in presence of the Eucharist; and thus, as upon the first Easter Day when Jesus Himself stood in the midst, the risen Lord, veiled in His Holy Sacrament, gives His solemn Benediction, and, as the *Pastor et Episcopus animarum*, bestows upon His people the Blessing of Peace.

Thus it is evident, from the consideration of the bearing of this rubric upon the Post-Communion, that the principle of reserving the Lord's Body for Eucharistic intercession, worship, and benediction, in union with the oblation of the holy Sacrifice, is

---

Council of Toledo (cited by Bona), is as follows: "Some priests, after the Lord's Prayer has been said, immediately communicate, and afterwards give the Blessing to the people, which we hereupon forbid; but after the Lord's Prayer and the mystical union of the bread and the cup (*conjunctionem panis et calicis*) let the Benediction of the people follow."—*Ibid.* This mystical union of the Lord's body and blood is a usage, it may be observed, which comes down to us from primitive times; it is enjoined in the Liturgy of S. James, in the very ancient Roman Order, and in other missals. *Cf.* Bona, *Rerum Lit.* lib. ii. cap. xv.

thereby intrinsically recognised. Moreover, when we consider the Eucharistic teaching of the eminent prelates who bequeathed to us this rubric, as recorded in their works, and the fidelity with which they witnessed to the traditional faith and worship of the Church, even unto imprisonment, exile, and martyrdom itself, we cannot but reasonably conclude that this recognition of our Lord's sacramental presence, as the consecrating principle of the Divine Liturgy, was intentionally restored. Even if otherwise, the fact of this restoration is all the more remarkable, in wonderfully illustrating the overruling providence of God and the perpetual guidance of that Holy Spirit Who animates the Body of Christ.

CHAPTER IV.

RESERVATION OF THE EUCHARIST ENJOINED BY THE
ECCLESIASTICAL LAW OF ENGLAND.

IN proceeding to the next part of our subject, we would commence by adducing Bishop Gibson's testimony to the great authority of the Provincial Constitutions made from time to time in Synods of the Province of Canterbury,[1] which although they "could have no *direct* influence or authority beyond the limits thereof, yet were they copied after in the Province of York, and seem to have been received there as the ecclesiastical laws of the English Church; especially since the time they were illustrated with a large and learned commentary by the famous Canonist, William Lyndwood."[2]

"Next to the solemn judgments of law," says Bishop Gibson, "are the Commentaries of Lynd-

[1] *Cf. Codex Juris Ecclesiastici Anglicani*, by Edmund Gibson, D.D., Archdeacon of Surrey, Rector of Lambeth, and Chaplain to his Grace the Lord Archbishop of Canterbury; subsequently Bishop of London. Dedicated to Archbishop Tenison (London, 1713). Pref. p. x.

[2] William Lyndwood was made Dean of the Arches by Archbishop Chicheley, *temp.* Henry V. He died, Bishop of S. David's, in 1446, and was buried at Westminster.

wood and John de Athon; the first upon the Provincial, the second upon the Legatine, Constitutions; whose authority (especially that of the first) is greatly regarded in the Courts of Civil and Canon Law not only as the opinions of persons eminently learned in both Laws, but chiefly as they are witnesses of the practice of the Church of England in their respective ages. Which practice, in very many cases, having continued the same, and been derived down to the present age upon *their* evidence and authority, their rules are become, in effect, the *Common Law of the Church*, and in that respect deserve great regard not only in the Spiritual, but also in the Temporal, Courts."[1]

1. The continued legality of the Provincial Constitutions is expressly enacted by Parliament in the well-known Act, 25 Hen. VIII. cap. 19:—

"Provided also, That such Canons, Constitutions, Ordinances, and Synodals Provincial, being already made, which be not contrariant nor repugnant to the laws, statutes, and customs of this realm, nor to the damage or hurt of the king's prerogative royal, shall now still be used and executed as they were afore the making of this Act."[2]

---

[1] *Cf.* Gibson's *Codex*, Preface, p. xii.

[2] This most important clause was added by way of rider in the House of Lords, and to it was appended a provision that the ancient Canon Law should be thus used and enforced until such time as it should be reviewed and determined by a commission of thirty-two persons, appointed for this purpose, according to this Act. "To Henry," as Dr. Lingard observes, "it was sufficient that he possessed the power of modifying the Ecclesiastical Laws at pleasure; that power he never thought proper to exercise; and the consequence has been that

Upon which Bishop Gibson observes that "this clause adds a parliamentary authority or enaction to all our own Canons and Constitutions which are not repugnant to the laws, statutes, and customs of this realm, nor to the damage or hurt of the king's prerogative royal." And further adds, in commenting upon the words, "as they were afore the making of this Act,"—"This shews of what consequence it is to preserve and examine our Ecclesiastical Records," here referred to, "in order to the support of ecclesiastical authority; since from these, and these alone, it can be made to appear on all occasions that it is entitled to the additional strength not only of Common, but likewise of Statute, Law."[1]

In like manner Bishop Cosin, in his *Notes upon the Ornaments Rubric*, comments as follows:—

"And these ornaments of the Church which by former laws, not then abrogated, were in use by virtue of the statute 25 Henry VIII., and for them the Provincial Constitutions are to be consulted, such as have not been repealed, standing then in the second year of King Edward VI., and being still in force by virtue of this rubric and act of parliament."[2] (*i.e.* 25 Henry VIII.)

Thus it is evident that the Provincial Constitutions are to be regarded as having statutory authority in virtue of this Act, and (subject to the limitations

in virtue of the additional clause the spiritual courts," and with them the Canon Law, which it is their function to administer, "have existed down to the present time."—*History of England*, by John Lingard, D.D., vol. vi. p. 204 (London, 1838.)

[1] *Cf.* Bishop Gibson's *Codex*, vol. ii. p. 985.
[2] *Cf.* Cosin's Works, vol. v. p. 439.

therein defined) are therefore still binding, since no length of non-observance can override the enactments of Statute Law.[1]

In illustration of this principle—that the Provincial Constitutions (notwithstanding temporary disuse) are our authoritative guide in matters of ecclesiastical discipline and observance—we would refer to Canon 81 of the Convocation of Canterbury in 1603, which is based upon the recognition of this principle, and provides that ancient ordinances and customs are to be observed still. This Canon ordains that:—

"According to a former Constitution, too much neglected in many places, we appoint, That there shall be a Font of Stone in every Church or Chapel where Baptism is to be ministred; the same to be set in the Ancient usual places. In which only Font the Minister shall baptize publicly."[2]

The "former Constitution" (*prisca Constitutione* in the Latin version) here referred to is undoubtedly that of Archbishop Edmund in 1236:—

"Baptisterium habeatur in qualibet Ecclesia Baptismali lapideum, vel aliud competens, quod decenter co-operiatur, et reverenter observetur, et in alios usus non convertatur."[3]

[1] *Cf. History of the Reformation*, by the late Rev. J. H. Blunt, M.A., p. 229.

[2] The original Latin version of this Canon is as follows: "Prout cautum est prisca Constitutione, hodie in quibusdam partibus neglectius habita: statuimus et ordinamus, ut in omni Ecclesia et Capella, ubi Baptismus administrari consuevit, Baptisterium ex lapide in loco antiquitus usitato statuatur: in quo duntaxat Ministris licebit Infantes publice Baptizare." *Cf.* Bishop Sparrow's *Collection of Articles, Canons, and Constitutions Ecclesiastical* (London, 1684).

[3] It is true that Bishop Gibson (apparently by an oversight) regards

In concluding this part of our argument in defence of the practice of reserving the Blessed Sacrament upon the ground that it is still enjoined by the Ecclesiastical Law, it ought to be stated that, in accordance with the provision of the statute (25 Henry VIII.) above referred to, a commission was empowered to examine and to revise the ancient Canon Law, and that a revised code of discipline, known as the *Reformatio Legum*, was the result of this commission.

This measure was rendered abortive in the first place by the premature death of Edward VI., and subsequently by the resolute determination of Queen Elizabeth not to sanction this proposed deviation from the canonical standard of ecclesiastical discipline

this "former Constitution" as referring to the Canons of 1571; but the words of the passage here referred to fall far short of the explicit directions contained in the Canon of 1603, which directions are, on the contrary, substantially identical with those of the Constitutions of 1236. This conclusion is further strengthened by the circumstance that the rubric of 1549, concerning the changing of the baptismal water, is evidently based upon the second part of the same Constitution of Archbishop Edmund. It is further to be observed that the words "*prisca Constitutione*," coupled with the phrase "in the ancient usual places," cannot (if words have any meaning) be regarded as simply referring to directions issued in the previous generation, but must necessarily refer to the Constitutions and customs of antiquity. It is, however, most probable that the direction of 1571—particularly in its closing words, which provide that "the sacred font" may be decently and honourably cared for (*decenter et munde conservetur*)—is itself based upon the "former Constitution" of 1236 (being, in fact, an intermediate link between the canonical discipline of earlier and later times), and that it thus affords additional evidence of the continued vitality of the ancient Constitutions of the Province of Canterbury.

In this respect the action of the Queen was entirely consistent with her determination to maintain the ancient standard of ritual and ceremonial in the service of the Church. In the Act of Uniformity, passed at the beginning of her reign, Elizabeth secured the addition of the well-known clause:—

"That such ornaments of the Church and of the ministers thereof shall be retained, and be in use, as was in this Church of England by the authority of Parliament in the second year of the reign of King Edward the Sixth, until other order shall be therein taken, etc."

Upon which Bishop Cosin observes,—"The Parliament thought fit not to continue this last order (of the fifth year of King Edward), but to restore the first again (of his second year); which, since that time, was never altered by any other law, and therefore it is still in force at this day."[1]

Thus in the Act of Uniformity, as in the twenty-fifth of Henry VIII. (which gave statutory force to the ancient Constitutions) provision was made for future revision; but in both instances the Queen resolutely set her face against any further alteration touching the canonical standard of discipline or of ceremonial observance; while at the same time many of the bishops, who were in sympathy with an alien system largely imported from Geneva, brought

[1] *Cf.* Bishop Cosin's *Notes on the Common Prayer*, Third Series, vol. v. p. 440.

in unauthorised innovations both in worship and discipline.

The Advertisements of Archbishop Parker, intended no doubt to stem the rising tide of irreverence and irregularity which threatened to destroy all order and decency in ecclesiastical administration, were commanded as a temporary measure "as rules in some part of discipline concerning decency, distinction, and order *for the time*,"[1] but not as introducing a permanent modification of the ancient standard of ceremonial enjoined in the Act of Uniformity.

But although neither the Advertisements of Archbishop Parker nor the *Reformatio Legum* possessed statutory authority, both introduced a deflection from the ancient Order of this Church and Realm, and to a great extent formed the basis of "ecclesiastical proceedings," which not only disfigured and degraded the Church, stripped religion of its beauty, and alienated the people in the reign of Elizabeth, but in their far-reaching consequences have well-nigh thrust out the old traditions, and interposed an effectual break in the continuity of that canonical discipline and observance which had hitherto prevailed.

A clean sweep was made of the ornaments of the Church and the Eucharistic vestments of the clergy, in flagrant violation of the law which

[1] *Cf.* Preface to the Advertisements of 1564.

commanded their retention and use, while the Provincial Constitutions, which by another statute were ordered "still to be used and executed," became virtually a dead letter, as evidenced by the fact that (so far as the writer of this Treatise has ascertained) no edition of the Constitutions was issued from the time of Archbishop Warham until 1677, when the present standard edition was published at Oxford with the *imprimatur* of the Vice-Chancellor of the University.[1]

No wonder, therefore, that the reservation of the Eucharist in our churches for the sick and dying, as enjoined in these Constitutions and confirmed by the additional authority of Statute Law, has in later times been regarded as appertaining to a foreign communion, but as being no part of our Catholic heritage in the venerable *Ecclesia Anglicana*; whereas, as we shall now proceed to shew, this primitive usage is explicitly enjoined by the ecclesiastical laws of this realm.

2. The Constitution of the Province of Canterbury, published by Archbishop Peccham in 1281, has never been repealed; to this day it stands among the Canons which, by the Act of 1534, are ordered "still to be used and executed." It dates from a time anterior to the decay of religion in the

---

[1] A small pocket edition, in fact a clergyman's *Vade-mecum*, containing the text of the Constitutions, but without the commentaries of Lyndwood, and now in the author's possession, was published in Queen Mary's reign, dedicated to Cardinal Pole.

fourteenth and fifteenth centuries; its object is to provide that the Sacrament of the Eucharist be reserved with becoming reverence and honour in every parish church, to be always in readiness for the communion of the sick; its phraseology, it is true, is characteristic of a by-gone age, but in substance it will be found to supply an effectual remedy for certain of the growing spiritual needs of our own time.

The first part of this Constitution is as follows:—

"Dignissimum Eucharistiæ Sacramentum Præcipimus de cætero taliter custodiri, ut in qualibet Ecclesia Parochiali fiat Tabernaculum, cum clausura decens et honestum, secundum Curæ magnitudinem et Ecclesiæ facultates, in quo ipsum Dominicum corpus non in bursa vel loculo propter comminutionis periculum nullatenus collocetur, sed in Pyxide pulcherrima lino candidissimo interius adornata; ita quod sine omni diminutionis periculo facile possit extrahi et imponi. Quod quidem venerabile Sacramentum omni die Dominica præcipimus innovari. Sacerdotes autem in custodia Eucharistiæ negligentes puniri præcipimus, secundum regulam Concilii generalis; et gravius, si in negligentia perseverent." [1]

This Constitution therefore enjoins that the most honourable Sacrament of the Eucharist be cared for in such sort, that in every parish church there be a decent tabernacle[2] with canopy (or other suitable

[1] *Cf.* Lyndwood's *Provinciale, seu Constitutiones Angliæ* (Oxoniæ, 1679), p. 248. Also Bp. Gibson's *Codex Juris Ecclesiastici Anglicanæ* (London, 1713), vol. i. p. 464.

[2] In England the Blessed Sacrament was commonly reserved in a tabernacle (often in the form of a dove) dependent from a canopy over the high altar; thus at Durham:—" Within the said quire, over the high altar, did hang a rich and most sumptuous canapie for the Blessed

protection) according to the greatness of the cure and the means of the church, in which the Lord's Body may conveniently be placed in a fair pyx lined with linen, whence it may easily be removed; but on no account is it to be laid up in a burse or other small receptacle whereby it might be endangered. And further, that this venerable Sacrament be renewed every Lord's day.

Before proceeding to the special directions for the reverent ministration of the Sacrament to the sick, which form the subject of the Second Part of

Sacrament to hang within it, ... whereon did stand a pelican, all of silver, upon the height of the said canapie, very finely gilded, giving her bloud to hir younge ones, in token that Christ did give His Blood for the sinns of the world; and it was goodly to behold for the Blessed Sacrament to hang in; and a marveilous fair Pix that the holy Blessed Sacrament did hang in, which was of most pure fine gold, most curiously wrought of goldsmith worke. And the white cloth that hung over the Pix was of verye fine lawne, all embroydered and wrought about with gold and red silke, and four great and round knopes of gold, marvelous and cunningly wrought, with great tassels of gold and red silke hanginge at them, and at the four corners of the white lawne cloth; and the crooke (that hung within the cloth) that the Pix did hang on was of gold, and the cords, that did draw it up and downe, were made of fine white strong silke." *Cf. The Rites of Durham*, written in 1593 (Surtees Society, 1842), p. 7. Lyndwood says that, although this English custom (*Consuetudo Anglicana*), may be commendable, because thereby the holy Sacrament is more readily seen as an object of veneration, yet upon other grounds it is not so suitable, because of the danger of irreverence. He therefore commends the custom which he had observed in foreign travel, where (as in Holland and Portugal) an honourable place near the altar (*e.g.* an Aumbrey) is specially ordered for that purpose, wherein the Eucharist may be safely and reverently enclosed, under the custody of the Parish-priest. *Cf. Provinciale*, p. 228, note (*e*).

this Constitution, we will consider the First Part, already given, in its historical, legal, and liturgical bearings.

(i) We find an important reference to the continued observance of this Constitution, concurrently with the use of the English Prayer Book, in the visitation of the Church of Durham by the devout and learned Tunstall in the year 1556.

When the aged Bishop—the friend of Erasmus, of Dean Colet, of Thomas Linacre (the eminent physician, by whose side he willed to be buried at S. Paul's), of Card. Fisher, and Sir Thomas More—was restored to his diocese after his imprisonment in the Tower during the latter half of the reign of Edward VI., he found certain irregularities in his Cathedral which called for reform.

The twelve Prebendaries of Durham at that time were, for the most part, those who had been first upon the foundation in 1541, when Hugh Whitehead,[1] the last Prior, became the first Dean, and several of the principal officers in the monastery

---

[1] Hugh Whitehead, S.T.P. of Durham College, Oxford, was one of the leading ecclesiastics of the day. He was made Prior of Durham in 1524, and presided over the Cathedral Church, first as Prior and then as Dean, until his death in 1551. He was distinguished not only by his corporate spirit in repairing the houses appertaining to the Deanery, but by "the white flower of a blameless life." "*In eleemosynis erat abundans, in puritate vitæ laudabilis. Hic in omni vita sua se Dei religioni conformem dedit; totus namque erat deditus amori divino.*" *Cf. Hist. Dunelm. Scriptores Tres.* pp. 154, 155 (Surtees Society, 1839).

were appointed to the newly-constituted Prebendal-stalls in the Cathedral.

It is not surprising, therefore, that few changes had been made in the Church of Durham, especially when it is remembered that Tunstall's faithful Suffragan, Thomas Sparke, Bishop of Berwicke and Prebendary of the Third Stall (formerly Chamberlain of the Abbey and Prior of Lindisfarne), had remained at his post during the enforced absence of the diocesan, although he too was threatened with deprivation.[1] But the head of the Chapter, from 1551 (after the death of Dr. Whitehead) to 1553, was Dean Horne, who was more advanced in the direction of Reform than his brethren among the Prebendaries. It is recorded that "he could never endure the ancient Monuments, Acts, or Deeds that

---

[1] Thus we find Dudley, Lord Northumberland, in his letter to Cecil of October 28th, 1552, saying:—" The Suffrecan, who ys placed without the Kinges Majesties auctorite, and allso hath a great lyvinge, nat worthy of yt, may be removyd, being nether precher, lernyd, nor honest man. And the same lyving, with a little more to the value of a hondreth marke, will serve for the erection of a bischop within New Castell. The sayd Soverycan ys so pervers a man, and of so evyll qualities, that the contry aborth him. He ys most metist to be removed from that offyce and from thos partyes. Thus may his Majestie place godly ministers in thies offyces as ys aforsayd, and reserve to his crowne 2000 li. a yere of the best landes within the north partes of his realme. . . . . Scribled in my bedd as yll at ease as I have byn moche in all my lyffe. Your assured frend— NORTHU'BBLAND." No words need be added to this estimate, thus prompted by mercenary motives, to establish the fair fame of the Bishop of Berwick. *Cf. Memoirs of Ambrose Barnes* (Merchant of Newcastle), Appendix, pp. 269, 270 (Surtees Society, 1866).

gave any light to true religion."[1] Certainly he destroyed the history of S. Cuthbert, depicted in glass in the cloister windows, and his ancient monument, likewise in the cloisters. Dean Horne also pulled down the parclose-screens which formerly enclosed the Choir, and thus exposed the Altar and the Blessed Sacrament (as Bishop Ridley had done at S. Paul's) to the irreverent intrusion of heretics who, as we learn from this visitation of Bishop Tunstall, "in the late most evil time, when the faith of Christ was shaken, feared not even to lay wicked hands upon the Sacrament of the Lord's Body and Blood (placed over the Altar), which they impiously cast upon the ground and trampled under foot."[2]

Thus it is evident that the ancient usage (enjoined in the Canon Law) of reserving the Blessed Sacrament "over the High Altar," as aforetime, (*vide* previous note) was observed concurrently with the use of the English Prayer Book, certainly in the latter part of the reign of Edward VI., when it was only interrupted (we are not told that it was discontinued) by the lawless violence of fanatics who undertook the self-imposed work of purifying the churches. This is an important fact which

---

[1] *Cf. Antiquities of Durham Abbey*, 1767, p. 69. Also *Rites of Durham*, p. 65.

[2] *Cf. Hist. Dunelm. Scriptores Tres.* Appendix, cccclvii. VISITATIO ECCLES. DUNELM. MDLVI. (Surtees Society, 1839).

disposes by anticipation of the opinion first broached by Wheatley in 1720 :—

"That, though anciently it was usual for the ministers to reserve some part of the consecrated Elements, either in the church or at their houses, to be always in a readiness for any who should want to receive before the time came to consecrate again; yet after the Reformation it was never allowed to reserve them longer than that day on which they were consecrated, nor indeed to reserve them at all, unless the curate knew beforehand that some sick person was that day to be visited."[1]

At the same time it also adds another link to the chain of evidence in support of the Anglican authority for the continuous Reservation of the Blessed Sacrament.

For, let it be granted that the rubric of 1549 provided merely for occasional reservation, it by no means follows that it thereby superseded the ancient practice which then rested upon the basis of Canon, Common, and Statute Law; on the contrary, the absence of any explicit prohibition, coupled with historical evidence, and the fact that some latitude is permitted under this rubric (inasmuch as the private celebration for the sick depends upon the curate "not being otherwise letted with the public service, or any other just impediment,") would seem to indicate that, while occasional reservation might be regarded as a sufficient compliance with the new provisions of the law, the observance of the older custom in nowise contravened the

[1] *Cf. Illustration of the Common Prayer*, by Charles Wheatley, M.A. (London, 1728), p. 481.

spirit of that law, inasmuch as the intention both of the Constitution of 1281 and of the rubric of 1549 was to provide for the communion of the sick and dying; an end, be it observed, which, under the present conditions of our social and ecclesiastical life, particularly in consideration of the needs of a largely increased population, is obviously more effectually secured by the traditional system of the Church than by what proved to be the merely tentative measure of 1549. While it must further be remembered that the effect of the omission of this rubric in 1552 was virtually to revive the unabated force of the ancient Canon, and that its restoration in the Latin Prayer Book of 1560 witnesses to the continued recognition of the primitive custom of reserving the Blessed Sacrament for the sick.

But to return to Bishop Tunstall's visitation. The Bishop directs that (as soon as conveniently may be) the choir-screens are to be so re-constructed that the people (save in time of divine service) may be excluded from the entrance and circuit of the Choir; as in the great church of S. Paul's, London, where (although the Nave is at all times open to all, even out of service-time) the Choir and its ambulatory always remain closed, except during the celebration of divine Offices.[1]

[1] A rule which, both in respect of the restored freedom now permitted in the open Nave, and of proper restrictions in reverently

Moreover, lest the heinous sacrilege of profaning the Holy Mysteries should again be attempted, the Bishop ordains (in words which recall the Constitution of Archbishop Peccham and the suggestions contained in Lyndwood's Commentary, already noticed) that "according to the sacred Canons the Sacrament of the Body and Blood of our Lord Jesus Christ should hereafter be reserved under safe custody in a decent tabernacle, either of stone or of wood and iron, over against the High Altar, of sufficient size in construction and workmanship as conveniently to receive the sacred pyx containing the Holy Sacrament."[1]

guarding the Choir, is (we may thankfully note) observed, not only at S. Paul's, but probably in all our cathedrals; and indeed in the large number of parish churches, which always remain open both for the daily service and for private devotion.

[1] "Ad hæc, quia nuper, perversissima hac tempertate, labefactata Christi fide, nonnulli heretici non modo reliqua sacramenta spernere sed manus etiam sceleratas in sacramentum corporis et sanguinis Domini super altare positum nefarie injicere et in terram projectum pedibus conculcare non sunt reveriti, ne de cetero tam immane facinus facile a pestilentibus hereticis attentari possit providere volentes, secundum sacros canones statuimus sacramentum corporis et sanguinis Domini nostri Jesu Christi in decenti tabernaculo, vel ex lapide vel ex ligno et ferro, tantæ amplitudinis sic construendo et fabrefaciendo, ut sacram pixidem in qua reconditur sacramentum commode recipere possit super summum altare, sub salva custodia seris et clavibus firmanda in futurum recondatur, ut non facile tabernaculum illud vel effringi aut sacramentum a prophanis hereticis auferri seu vim pati et ludibrio haberi in posterum possit. Ad quod tabernaculum decentissime et tutissime fabrefaciendum nos pro virili nostra expensas libenter ex animo subituri sumus." VISITATIO ECCLES. DUNELM. MDLVI. [in the Registry of the Dean and Chapter]. *Cf. Hist. Dunelm. Scriptores Tres*, p. cccclvi. (Surtees Society, 1839).

This ordinance, as we have seen, was strictly in accordance with the Ecclesiastical Law, as enjoined by the ancient Canons and sanctioned by Statute Law. We have also seen that this law remains unchanged; for although the Act of 25 Hen. VIII. was repealed under Philip and Mary, it was revived by the statute passed in the first year of Elizabeth, which enacts that it "shall stand and be in full force and strength, to all intents, constructions, and purposes."[1]

The question therefore arises:—How comes it to pass that this order for the reverent care of the Blessed Sacrament of the Lord's Body and Blood, so entirely in accordance with the provisions of Canon and Statute Law (as revived in the first year of Elizabeth), has been persistently set aside in open disobedience to the law?

In order to answer this enquiry it will be convenient to supplement what has already been advanced upon the general question by briefly indicating the course of contemporary events in relation to the Diocese of Durham.

Elizabeth ascended the throne Nov. 17th, 1558.

---

[1] This re-enforcement of the ancient Canons in all probability explains the action of the Queen in refusing her sanction to the *Reformatio Legum*, notwithstanding the request of Convocation in 1562 and the efforts made in Parliament in 1571:—facts, be it observed, which materially strengthen the argument in support of the continued force of the ancient Canon Law. *Cf.* Bishop Gibson's *Codex Juris Ecclesiastici Anglicani*, vol. ii. pp. 976, 991 (London, 1713).

From Bishop Tunstall's Register we learn that Holy Orders were as usual administered at Bishop Auckland, Dec. 17th, 1558, and May 25th, 1559.

Within a month from this latter date, *viz.* on the Nativity of S. John Baptist, the English service was restored.

In August of that same year we find Bishop Tunstall writing to his "veray lovinge frende, Sir William Cicill, Knight, Chief Secretary unto the Queenes Highnes," to request an interview with Elizabeth respecting matters ecclesiastical, adding:—

"And where I do understande, out of my diocesse, of a warnyng for a visitacion to be had there, thies shall be t' advertise your mastership, that, albeit I wolde be as glad to serve the Quenes Highnes, and to set forwardes all her affayres to her contentacion as any subjecte in her realme, yet, if the same visitacion shall procede to suche ende in my diocesse of Durham as I do playnly se to be set furthe here in London, as in pullinge downe of altares, defacing of churches by takinge awaye of the crucifixes, I can not in my conscience consent to it, beinge pastor there, bicause I can not myself agree to be a sacramentary, nor to have any newe doctryne taught in my diocesse, whereof I thought mete t' advertise your mastership, humbly beseechinge the same not to thinke me thereunto moved, eyther for any frowardness, malice, or contempte, but onely bicause my conscience will not suffer me to receyve and allowe any doctrine in my diocesse other than Catholike. As knoweth Almyghtye Jesu, who ever preserve your mastership to his pleasure and yoyrs. From London, the xixth of Auguste, 1559. Your masterships humble most assured loving frende. CUTH. DURESME."[1]

Notwithstanding the well-known convictions of Bishop Tunstall thus dutifully but firmly expressed, he was on the ninth of September following commissioned, with five other bishops, to confirm the election of Dr. Matthew Parker to the Metropolitical See of Canterbury (then vacant by the death of Cardinal Pole), and to proceed to consecration. This commission was not executed in consequence of the canonical difficulty felt by three (if not four) of the prelates in consecrating an Archbishop-elect who was a married man; an objection which was shared by the Queen, who, though nominating Parker to the primacy, out of respect for the memory of her mother (to whom he had been chaplain) and in recognition of his own merit, would never agree to the revival of the Act of Edward VI. legalising the marriages of the Clergy. "They should be content," the Queen said, "if she connived at them; for she would never sanction them."[2]

[1] *Cf. Memoirs of Ambrose Barnes*, Illustrative Documents, p. 281. Another copy was addressed to Sir Thos. Perry, Treasurer of the Queen's Household, which thus affords additional evidence of the profound anxiety experienced by Bishop Tunstall respecting the threatened visitation.

[2] *Cf.* Dr. Lingard's *History of England*, vol. vii. p. 260.

But Elizabeth could ill brook any disobedience to her wishes, and therefore the prelates (among whom was Tunstall) who thus declined to consecrate Parker, upon their refusal to take the Oath of Supremacy, were deprived, probably in October, 1559.

Parker, it should be remembered, had much in common with Cuthbert Tunstall; both were distinguished by moderation, piety, and learning; both were in favour of Catholic reform, though Tunstall was more conservative in this respect, and less disposed than Parker to acquiesce in measures of liturgical revision. But under the over-mastering force of the reaction against Catholicism, caused by the cruelties which (in mistaken zeal for the ancient faith) were perpetrated in the reign of Mary, combined with the intolerance of fanaticism and of Genevan reform, all focussed in London upon the accession of Elizabeth, Parker found himself in a position of exceptional difficulty, which (under the aggravation of physical weakness) probably carried him further in assenting to innovations, either than his own judgment warranted, or the Queen and her Chief Secretary Cecil desired.[1] Certain it is that,

---

[1] We are told that the Queen, Cecil, and others were in favour of restoring the Prayer Book of 1549; but that, in deference to the majority of the Commission, that of 1552 was eventually adopted, though with certain important additions and alterations; *e.g.* the Ornaments rubric, carrying with it the Eucharistic vestments of 1549 and enjoining the retention of the *Ornamenta* and ancient ceremonial,

like Tunstall, Parker contemplated with dismay the results of the proposed visitation. On Nov. 6th, 1559, he thus writes to Cecil:—"God keep us from such a visitation as Knox has attempted in Scotland."

Parker and Tunstall had indeed sufficient cause for disquietude in the sacrilege and destruction which had been perpetrated by fanatical violence in the churches of London; but happily such irregularities were by no means universal; there had been no Marian persecution in the North, consequently there was no anti-Catholic reaction in Yorkshire,

---

was prefixed to the *Order for Morning Prayer;* it was also ordered that "the chancels shall remain as they have done in times past." The ancient *formula* in administering Holy Communion was restored and prefixed to the words which had been substituted for it in 1552. The Declaration respecting *kneeling at the Holy Sacrament*, which appeared to deny "any real and essential presence there being of Christ's natural Flesh and Blood," was omitted; and in the Calendar (prefixed in 1561) the Black-letter holidays were for the most part restored. Parker being unable on account of sickness to attend the meetings of this Commission, Edmund Guest, who afterwards became Bishop of Rochester and then of Salisbury, (who in 1562 revised the Twenty-eighth Article) was appointed to act as Parker's deputy. Thus the revision of 1559 was altogether in the direction of maintaining the traditional Faith and Order of the Church, though Catholics still had grave cause for dissatisfaction in the preference given to the book of 1552, in the illegal destruction of altars and the dishonour done to Christ's holy Mysteries; hence the Queen's Injunctions to prevent these irregularities and to restore "the usual bread and wafer, which served for the use of the private Mass." Also the renewed recognition in the Latin Prayer Book of 1560 of the primitive custom of reserving the Eucharist for the Sick, and of prayers for the Faithful Departed, particularly in the provision for Celebration at Funerals, then restored from the Prayer Book of 1549.

5—2

Lancashire, the Diocese of Durham, or in that of Carlisle, upon the accession of Elizabeth.

"The Bishoprick of Durham (saith Fuller) had halcyon days of ease and quiet, under God and good Cuthbert Tunstall, the Bishop thereof. A learned man, of a sweet disposition, rather devout to follow his own than cruel to persecute the conscience of others."[1]

Hence it need occasion no surprise to find the Duke of Norfolk writing to Cecil from Newcastle, Jan. 10th, 1560, as follows:—

"Forasmuch as I do find this town and country hereabout far out of order in matters of religion, and the altars standing still in the churches, contrary to the Queen's Majesty's proceedings, it shall be well done that you procure her Majesty's commands to be addressed to the Dean of Durham, and such others as shall be thought meet there, authorising them to see these things reformed in such sort as shall answer to the advancement of God's true religion, and the confirmation of the Queen's Majesty's godly zeal thereto."[2]

---

[1] *Cf.* Appendix to *Memoirs of Ambrose Barnes*, p. 280. Bishop Tunstall passed to his rest on Nov. 18th, 1559, at Lambeth Palace, where (after his deprivation) he ended his days in the "free custody" of his friend, Dr. Matthew Parker, then Elect of Canterbury, at whose charge he was honourably buried in the chancel of the Church of Lambeth, "*ubi primo consecratus fuit Episcopus.*" A fair marble stone, bearing a laudatory epitaph, was placed over his grave. This however has unfortunately disappeared, probably in the great rebellion, or possibly in the so-called restoration of Lambeth Church, where no memorial now remains of one who, in most critical times, was a distinguished ornament of the English episcopate, who is described by the historian as,—"*in omni vitæ genere præclarus Præsul.*" *Cf. Hist. Dunelm. Scriptores Tres.* p. 156.

[2] *Cf.* Sharp's Rebellion, 377, quoted in Appendix to *Ambrose Barnes*, p. 283. From the above extract it would appear that even the Duke of Norfolk had adopted the anti-Catholic policy of Somerset and

It is therefore evident that up to this date, notwithstanding the Queen's visitation, no alterations had been made either in the Ornaments of the Church or of the ministers thereof; "the altars" were "standing still in the churches," consequently the tabernacles for the reservation of the Blessed Sacrament were still in their usual place, both at Durham and York (*vide infra*), Newcastle "and country hereabout"; for we find no evidence of any order for their removal, or indeed of their irregular destruction; the Ecclesiastical Law enjoining the Reservation of the Eucharist had again received statutory confirmation;[1] under the English rite of 1559 it was ordered that "the chancels shall remain as they have done in times past"; and there was no direction in the Book of Common Prayer which bore even the semblance of prohibiting the practice of Reservation.

We have corroborative testimony to the continuance of the accustomed order in the fact that little or no change was made in the great Metropolitical Church of York until after Matthew Hutton became Dean in 1567; he was in sympathy with the ultra-reforming party, and removed the altars which had hitherto remained standing. The taber-

Northumberland in the reign of Edward VI. Like them, he was now urging the unconstitutional exercise of royal authority, in order to coerce those who were invested with ecclesiastical jurisdiction to bring about illegal changes in matters of religion.

[1] *Cf.* p. 63.

nacle also, which (as we learn from the Account Rolls) had probably been made in 1556, was apparently taken down at this time, for in the Roll of 1567 we find the entry :—" For the paynted clothe over the communion table, 7d." Also, " for making playne and workyng over with whyte the places where the altar stood, . . ." and for taking " downe of the almeries in the highe quere, 4d."[1]

Upon the whole, therefore, the records of history lead to the conclusion that, as the changes at York were inaugurated by a new Dean (actuated by Puritan prejudices rather than by the Catholic temper) in 1567, so likewise no change was made at Durham, touching the Altar and the accustomed Reservation of the Blessed Sacrament, until the Calvinistic and Iconoclastic Whittingham was intruded

---

[1] *Cf. Fabric Rolls of York Minster*, pp. 113, 114 (Surtees Society, 1858). Before 1556 the Sacrament had been reserved in a pyx suspended over the High Altar as at Durham. In the Register of S. Thomas' Hospital, York, we find the following entry:—"6 May, 1560.—Md. also, that a grene sylke vestement, wth albe and appurtenaunces, bequethyd to this hospytall by Sir William Pynder, Clerke, emonges othyr thynges, in his testament, is broght in this day; and also a pyx of vyvery (ivory) wth a lytle white canaby and iiij knopes of sylver and gylte with reade tasshells." (See previous note respecting the pyx and the canopy at Durham.) *Cf. The Guild of Corpus Christi, York*, p. 307. (Surtees Society, 1871.) From the above Register it would appear that the chapel of this hospital remained as in times past, with its legal *Ornamenta*, until Feb. 4th, 1578, when it was " Agreed, that the glasse wyndowes of this hospitall hows shalbe with all convenyent spede transposed; and that all pictures and challices and hoastes . . . . . shalbe taken forth and defased." *Ibid.* p. 310. Then vestment and pyx would no doubt disappear in this wanton destruction of memorials of the old religion.

Enjoined by the Ecclesiastical Law. 71

into the Deanery (although a layman) in 1563. Then indeed the work of demolition, spoliation, and desecration began which so deeply stirred men's minds and contributed to the calamitous rising of 1569; the cathedral and dependent churches were defaced, the Altars were thrown down and cast out, the crucifixes broken, and the tabernacles destroyed.

Thus it has come to pass that Bishop Tunstall's order for the due observance of the sacred Canons concerning the reserving of the Holy Sacrament, set forth in Archbishop Peccham's Constitution, and confirmed by the authority of Statute Law, has been frustrated and forgotten, not because the law has been changed, but in consequence of the *anomia* which prevailed in the reign of Elizabeth.

(ii) With regard to the legal aspect of this question, it must in fairness be admitted that this Constitution which we are considering is regarded as obsolete by Bishop Gibson. Here, however, it is necessary for us to remember that by "obsolete" this learned Canonist would not lead us to conclude that this Constitution has therefore been *abrogated* by desuetude; but simply that, although *legally* in force, it has in consequence of a combination of circumstances become disused, as contrasted with laws which continue to be actively in force.

It is true indeed that Canon Law may be abrogated by desuetude or contrary custom, but it is also true that certain conditions are requisite in order that custom (*consuetudo*) may prevail against law.

These conditions are regarded by most modern Canonists as falling under two principal heads:

The custom must be reasonable; it must also possess sufficient legitimate prescription.

A custom which contravenes some "laudable practice of the whole Catholic Church of Christ,"[1] and thereby weakens the spirit and force of ecclesiastical discipline, cannot be regarded as *reasonable;* Nor can it be held that a merely local custom, such as the disuse of Reservation in England, can plead legitimate prescription, when it is remembered that the provincial episcopate gave no sign of any intention to abrogate the then existing law, at the time when it is assumed that the practice in question was prohibited, but on the contrary left on record a formal disclaimer of any such divergence from "the common order of the Church."[2]

And while on the one hand, in regard to persons, it may be admitted that the long-continued, though informal, sanction of a contrary custom by the provincial episcopate must be taken into account, both in estimating the gravity of non-observance and in reviving obedience to the precepts of the law; on

---

[1] *Cf.* Preface to the Book of Common Prayer.

[2] *Cf. Explanation of the Thirty-nine Articles*, by Bishop Forbes. Art. xxxiv.

Enjoined by the Ecclesiastical Law. 73

the other hand, as regards the law itself, it must be remembered that, inasmuch as it has always been legally binding, no lengthened prevalence of contrary custom can really impair the obligation of obedience to its commands.

Upon this point we have the important testimony of Bishop Cosin, quoted from Lyndwood:—

"Nam cum lex ista contineat præceptum, ergo eam non servans peccat, et ut transgressor puniendus est..... Unde nec consuetudo nec desuetudo excusare potest in hoc casu.... præsertim cum hæc legis clausula ab initio ligabat, nec tempus est modus tollendæ obligationis." [1]

In fact, Canonists hold that Ecclesiastical Law cannot be abrogated by desuetude save under very exceptional circumstances; for example, that the custom be not unreasonable nor contrary to the practice and discipline of the whole Church, nor such as would tend to spiritual laxity in the worship of God and ministration of the Sacraments; and further, that it be supported by legitimate prescription in the prevailing custom of the Christian world, and that those with whom it originated, and by whom it has been continued, be free from the imputation of heresy, or of ignorance, on the subject-matter of the law.

Much less can it be alleged that such law is abrogated when it is remembered that it is embodied in and supported by a distinct enactment of Statute

Cf. Notes upon the Common Prayer, Second Series, p. 184. Also *Provinciale*, lib. i. tit. 2, p. 13, note (*f*).

Law, concerning which it is an acknowledged principle (here in England) that it holds good until it be repealed.

This point has already been established in the first section of this chapter, concerning the continued legality of the Provincial Constitutions, as enacted by the 25th of Henry VIII. To what has been there stated it may here be added that, in reply to the argument from desuetude and the informal sanction of *non-user* on the part of the provincial episcopate, the late Dr. A. J. Stephens, Q.C., says very pertinently:—

"The irresistible answer is that neither the 'Governors in the Church' nor 'usage' can supersede the positive enactments of Statute Law." And again, "No custom, however confirmed, can supersede the Statute Law."[1]

---

[1] *Cf.* Dr. Stephens' book, *Notes, Legal and Historical, on the Book of Common Prayer*, vol. i. pp. 367, 368, 351, 39 .

The author is indebted to his friend the Rev. E. G. Wood, M.A., Vicar of St. Clement's, Cambridge, for the above reference, together with much valuable information contained in a paper *On the Abrogation of Canon Law by Desuetude*, communicated to the *Church Review* of August 16th, 1873, from which he cites the following:

(*a*) "What constitutes *irrationabilitas* in a custom? It is not necessary that the custom should *per se* be bad, for—'*Consuetudo potest esse irrationabilis etiam si* ex materia *mala non sit*' (Suarez, *De Legibus*, vii. 6, 11)."

"And unless it can clearly be shewn that," upon the grounds above given in the Text, "the custom is not irrational, no amount of universality, no length of time, can enable it to prevail over law."

(*b*) "As to those who bring in the custom. The consent" is necessary "of the major part of the community with respect to which

We must not, however, lose sight of the fundamental principle, so ably stated and clearly elucidated by Bishop Gibson, that:—

"The Statute Law, though reckoned the first in point of authority, comes properly in the last place when it is considered as part of the Ecclesiastical Law of the Church of England. For, as Canons were made from time to time to supply the defects of the *Common Law* of the Church, so were Statutes added to enforce both *Common* and *Canon* Law; and they are therefore to be considered as *supplemental* to both. The clergy, being devoted and consecrated to the immediate service of religion, have ever been the peculiar care of Christian States; who have expressed that care in providing for their quiet and security against oppressions and invasions of all kinds. And accordingly the greatest part of the Statutes made before the Reformation, which concern the Church and clergy, are directly levelled against violence committed upon their possessions or

the law to be abrogated was made. And so Suarez (vii. 6) says that *the Common Law of the Church must, in order to be abrogated by custom, be prescribed against by the custom of the whole Church.*"

" Again, those who induce the custom must be *bonâ fide* members of the Church. The custom of heretics cannot prevail *contra jus Ecclesiæ*."

"There must be a distinct intention to abrogate the law (*Prælectiones Jur. Can.* i. 20), and hence there must be a knowledge of the law on the part of those who induce the custom. A custom arising out of ignorance does not abrogate law; for—' *Consuetudo inducitur ex scientia non per errorem*' (Panormitanus, *in cap.* 'cum tanto,' n. 12)."

persons by the ministers of the king; and against the encroachments of the Temporal Courts upon the Spiritual Jurisdiction. In like manner, since the Reformation, the State hath interposed by many Acts, for the better ordering of the possessions of the Church and the more easy recovery of her just rights. And whereas, in the administration of discipline and correction of vice, the Church can go no further than spiritual censures; in this part also she hath been assisted from the State by additions of Temporal penalties; in cases which those censures would not easily reach, or in which they were like to prove ineffectual."

The following also, upon the proper function of the Temporalty in supporting, but in no wise superseding, the action of the Spiritualty, is too important to be omitted. Bishop Gibson continues:—

"But if these additional helps are *imposed* when there is no need of them (that is, where the ends may be attained as well, or better, in the present ecclesiastical way), or are given upon such terms as destroy or weaken the Ecclesiastical Jurisdiction, or transfer business of a spiritual nature from spiritual to temporal hands; in such cases the interpositions of the State either wholly cease to be real assistances to the Church, or at least the benefit which the Church might otherwise reap from them is greatly abated. The clergy themselves may well be presumed the best judges—what are the proper methods for promoting religion and the interest of the Church—in all kinds; how far their own strength will carry them in that way, and when it is that, in order to those ends, they *need* the assistance of the State. And therefore the greatest part of our ancient laws in favour of the Church and clergy were made upon special *petitions* of the clergy themselves to the king in Parliament; and we have already observed that Queen Elizabeth thought it no *unreasonable* message to the Commons in Parliament *that no bills concerning religion should be preferred or received there unless the same should be first considered and liked by the clergy.* . . . .

"In this point the constitution of the ecclesiastical body is not unlike the constitution of the *body* natural, in the case of which, its own strength is to be tried in the first place; and when it appears that Nature cannot do the work, then is the time for medicines to be prepared and administered by skilful hands, in such measures as Nature needs them, and in such methods as are most likely to assist her. But to put Nature out of her own course without cause, and to force upon her *unnecessary* assistances, is not the way to preserve, but to destroy, the constitution. Medicines (like other experiments) promise many things which they do not perform; or however they may seem, for the present, to make the work quick and short, it is frequently found in the end that it had been far better to have left Nature, though somewhat more *slow*, to do the work in her own way.

"So in our present case, if the helps which the Temporal Legislature affords the Church happen to be *unnecessary* or applied in an *undue* manner, they not only do no service, but a manifest disservice, to the Church,—by taking the suppression of vice out of the hands of the *Spiritualty* (whose proper province it is, and who are most like to pursue it), and putting it into the hands of the laity, who (to say no more) are generally too much taken up with secular cares and diversions to attend the work with those degrees of application which it deserves and requires."[1]

It is therefore to be remembered that the Reservation of the Eucharist, although confessedly enjoined by the Queen's Ecclesiastical Law, rests primarily upon immemorial custom and Catholic tradition, which may be properly regarded as expressing the Common Law of the Church; *i.e.* the *Jura non scripta*, the *Common Customs of the Spiritualty*. The Common Law has been regulated by the Canon Law set forth (here in England) in the Provincial Constitutions, "which have been made from time to time by ecclesiastical authority within this realm, whether before or since the Reformation."[2] These Constitutions have further been ratified by the sup-

---

[1] *Cf.* Bp. Gibson's *Codex*, I. xxx. [2] *Ibid.* I. xxix.

plemental authority of Statute Law; hence it follows (as affirmed by a resolution of both Houses of Parliament, cited by Lord Coke in the case of *Bird and Smith*):— "That when the Convocation make Canons concerning matters which properly appertain to them, and the king hath confirmed them, they are binding to the whole realm."[1]

Thus the primitive custom of reserving the Eucharist for the sick, notwithstanding temporary non-observance, is still legally binding as part of the established Order of this Church and realm, which does but affirm and enjoin the Common Law of the whole Church.

In illustration of the legal aspect of this question, it is further worthy of notice that in the *non-user* and revived observance of the Ornaments rubric we have a striking parallel to the disuse and eventual restoration (so greatly to be desired) of the Reservation of the Blessed Sacrament; a consideration which enables us to see the exact force of the term "obsolete" as applied to the Constitution of Archbishop Peccham. For instance, we find Bishop Gibson commenting as follows upon the clause in the Act of Uniformity of 1559, which provides that the Ornaments of the Church and the vestments of the clergy "shall be retained and be in use as . . . . in the second year of the reign of King Edward VI., until other order shall be taken therein;" "which

[1] Bp. Gibson's *Codex*, I. xxx.

other order (at least in the method prescribed by this Act) was never yet made; and therefore, *legally*, the Ornaments of ministers in performing divine service are the same now as they were in 2 Edw. VI."[1]

Nevertheless, the rubric of 2 Edw. VI. here referred to, which specifies the Ornaments of the ministers, then in use, and which (in virtue of the Act of 1559) continued to be legally in force, is noted as "obsolete,"[2] because the Ornaments enjoined therein had subsequently, in violation of the discipline and immemorial custom of the whole Church, been irregularly disused.

This meaning of the term "obsolete" as indicating actual *non-user*, but not implying abrogation by desuetude, is also plain from Bishop Cosin's Notes upon the Ornaments rubric; upon which this illustrious divine, to whom the leading part in the revision of the Prayer Book in 1661 was assigned by the Convocations of both provinces, comments as follows:—

"And therefore, according to this rubric, we are still bound to wear albs and vestments, as have been so long worn in the Church of God, *howsoever it is neglected*. For the disuse of these Ornaments we may thank them that came from Geneva, and in the beginning of Queen Elizabeth's reign, being set in places of government, suffered every negligent priest to do what him listed, so he would but profess a difference and opposition in all things (*though never so lawful otherwise*) against the Church of Rome, and the ceremonies therein used."[3]

[1] Bp. Gibson's *Codex*, I. 363. [2] *Ibid.* I. 472.
[3] *Cf. Notes on the Book of Common Prayer*, First Series, p. 42.

Again, in Cosin's Third Series of *Notes on the Common Prayer*, written when he was in middle life, and which may therefore be regarded as expressing his matured opinion upon the legal bearings of this question, after stating that the Act of Uniformity of 1559 restored the Ornaments of the second year of Edward VI., "which since that time was never altered by any other law, and therefore it is still in force at this day," he adds, as shewing the obligation of obedience to Ecclesiastical Law, which, "howsoever neglected" in practice, is not thereby abrogated :—

"And both bishops, priests, and deacons, that knowingly and wilfully break this order, are as hardly censured in the preface to this book concerning ceremonies as ever Calvin or Bucer censured the ceremonies themselves."[1]

So likewise this Constitution of Archbishop Peccham, enjoining the Reservation of the Blessed Sacrament in every parish church, resting, as it does, upon the *Jus Commune Ecclesiasticum* (*i.e.* upon the ancient custom and immemorial practice which are properly to be regarded as the Common Law of the whole Church,)[2] regulated by the Canon Law and supported by the supplemental authority of Statute Law, has always been legally in force, notwithstanding irrational and irregular *non-user*, and therefore is capable of being revived in practice, just

[1] *Cf.* Cosin's *Notes*, etc., Third Series, p. 440.
[2] *Cf.* Bishop Gibson's *Codex*, I. xxvii.

as the observance of the Ornaments rubric, which for a time was also regarded as "obsolete," but has now to a considerable extent been restored.

(iii) The direction that the Sacrament be renewed every Lord's day is worthy of particular notice, since it will be found, upon examination, to suggest certain important liturgical considerations.

Upon this part of the Constitution Lyndwood comments as follows:—

> "Every Sunday *at the least*. For upon other days the Sacrament may be renewed in case of urgent necessity; because the priest will always have the Eucharist in readiness for the sick. Nor is this contrary to the rule which forbids the reserving of several Hosts which may be left upon the Altar; for it is true that they ought not to be reserved for the convenience of those consecrating,[1] but for the needs of the dying. And that for such an end as this the Eucharist ought to be reserved."[2]

Thus it appears that, according to the Common Law of the Church of England, the Sacrament is to be reserved for one purpose, and only one; viz. the needs of the sick and dying; and that it ought not to be so reserved for a longer period than one week; "*quod Eucharistia non reservetur ultra unam hebdomadam.*"[3] But if any remain of that which was consecrated, over and above the actual needs of the

---

[1] This is evidently in harmony with, and may probably have suggested, the clause in the Scotch rubric of 1637:—"And to the end there may be little left, he that officiates is required to consecrate with the least."

[2] *Cf.* Lyndwood's *Provinciale*, lib. iii. tit. 26.

[3] *Ibid.* p. 248, note (o).

sick during the past week, or their probable needs in the coming week, it is ordered:—

"And if any remain of that which was consecrated, the priest and his ministers, that is to say, the deacon and sub-deacon, shall receive and consume the same."[1]

Here then we find the intermediate link between the primitive usage referred to by Pope Gelasius as an ancient custom in the Roman Church in the fifth age, and its survival among the *Cautelæ Missæ* appended to our English Communion Office (see Chap. III. Sec. 2, p. 35). Cosin and the orthodox clergy of the Caroline period, as we have already seen, deeply realised the need of a cautionary rubric, such as that which first took shape in the Scottish Liturgy of 1637, in order to guard against the "profanation of the holy Sacrament" (see Chap. II. pp. 9—12) arising from the Puritan abuse of treating the consecrated Elements as common food, either in taking "all that remained of the consecrated Bread and Wine itself home to their houses, there (to) eat and drink the same with their other common meats," or in tarrying "behind in the church, there with other people, in profane and common manner, to eat and to drink at the Lord's Table and in the House of God." Cosin, as we learn from his *Notes on the Book of Common Prayer*, was in the habit of referring to Lyndwood. Indeed, it would appear that the *Provinciale* was with him a

[1] *Ibid.* note (q).

recognised authority in all questions of ecclesiastical discipline. It is therefore not surprising to find him in the first place enjoining very positively that "if any remain of that which was consecrated, it shall not be carried out of the Church;"—just as Lyndwood had said with equal definiteness, "*non debent reservari ad opus consecratium*;"—and then falling back upon the old canonical rule for the reverent receiving of any that might not be needed for purposes of Communion.

Now, in order that we may duly estimate the bearing of this canonical rule (set forth in the provincial Constitutions) upon our present rubric, it is important that we should regard this question from the same point of view with the Revisers of 1661. In the first place therefore it must be remembered that although the primitive custom of reserving the Eucharist for the sick and dying had ceased to be generally observed in England, its ecclesiastical and statutory authority remained unchanged; moreover, it was not only enjoined in the Constitutions of Archbishop Peccham, ratified by Statute Law, but the rubrics of 1549 directing its observance had been incorporated in the then existing Latin Prayer Book of 1560; consequently, this ancient and canonical usage might at any time be adopted, and, under more favourable conditions of ecclesiastical life, be eventually restored. But, taking into account the abnormal state of things which had prevailed in England from the early part of Elizabeth's reign down to the Restoration, and which had culminated in the spiritual desolations caused by the great rebellion; when for nearly a hundred years the Eucharist had not been celebrated more than once a quarter in parish churches, or possibly once a month, and when the rubric enjoining Celebration "in Cathedral and Collegiate Churches and Colleges... *every Sunday at the least*" had become a dead letter; when the whole Church and nation were experiencing the evil results of the arbitrary measures, innovations, and reactionary changes of the previous century, which had so undermined the foundations of political and ecclesiastical life as to cause the temporary overthrow of the Church and Monarchy to be even possible;—it would have been utterly futile, nay, it would have imperilled the very restoration of order and worship which the rulers both in Church and State were striving to consolidate, if the bishops had enforced the rigorous observance of usages, which, though again enjoined (either explicitly or by implication), had for so long a period been neglected or forgotten.

Happily the Revisers have left on record in their Preface to the Book of Common Prayer a statement of the principles upon which they proceeded, from which we may learn both what alterations they rejected and what improvements they adopted in the fulfilment of that work which to this day is an enduring monument of their fidelity and moderation. On the one hand, they "rejected all such alterations as were either of dangerous consequence (as secretly striking at some established Doctrine or laudable Practice of the Church of England, or indeed of the whole Catholic Church of Christ)";—while on the other, they willingly assented to such alterations or additions "as seemed in any degree requisite or expedient ... for the better direction of them that are to officiate in any part of Divine Service, which is chiefly done in the Kalendars and Rubrics." Under neither of these heads is it possible to include the assumed prohibition of the "laudable practice" of reserving the Eucharist, then recognised and enjoined in the established Order of the Church of England from the earliest times, as "indeed of the whole Catholic Church of Christ." The scope and intention of this particular rubric (over and above the "general aim" set forth in the Preface of "the procuring of Reverence and exciting of Piety and Devotion in the Public Worship of God"), is therefore narrowed to "*the better direction of them that are to officiate*" in the Celebration of Holy Communion.

And so we come to the conclusion that under the guidance of a leader like Cosin, a prelate distinguished even among the Revisers of 1661 by his devotion, patristic learning, and liturgical knowledge, this cautionary rubric to secure reverence for the Blessed Sacrament, framed upon the provincial Constitution enjoining its reservation, was so worded as not only to meet the practical exigencies of the time, but to provide for the observance of the Common Law of the Church regulating such reservation,[1] when the Catholic rule of daily, or at least weekly, Celebration intended by the Church should eventually be restored.[2] Since it must be remembered that inasmuch as the Law directs that this venerable Sacrament is to "be renewed every Sunday at the least,"[3] its Reservation is implicitly forbidden except upon condition of its regular and frequent Celebration.

[1] Set forth in Lyndwood's Commentary, *vide supra*, p. 48.

[2] *Cf.* Cosin's Note upon the Order directing *that the Collect, Epistle, and Gospel, appointed for the Sunday, shall serve all the week after* [*except there fall some feast that hath his proper*]. "Which is so appointed, for that the epistle and gospel are to be read every day of the week, as every day there should be communion. If people be married upon the week-day, at that time by this book they are enjoined to receive; and so when women after child-birth are churched; or when men in cathedral churches (where they are enjoined it every Sunday at the least) shall desire to have communion on the week-day; that then the collect, epistle, and gospel shall be used which was appointed for the Sunday." *Notes upon the Common Prayer*, First Series, p. 16.

Also upon the rubric:—*And there shall be no celebration, etc., except there be a good number* [altered at the last Review in 1661 to *a convenient number*] *to communicate with the priest according to his discretion.*" "Better were it to endure the absence of the people than for the minister to neglect the usual and daily sacrifice of the Church, by which all people, whether they be there or no, reap so much benefit. And this was the opinion of my lord and master Dr. Overall." *Ibid.* p. 127.

[3] *Cf.* Provincial Constitution with Lyndwood's comment. *Provinciale*, p. 248.

So far indeed were those eminent divines and fathers of the Church from forbidding Reservation, that we owe it (under God) to their wisdom, knowledge, and foresight, that the leading characteristic and effect of their work of revision has been a marked and consistent advance towards the more perfect Catholicism of the early and undivided Church.

"Which way,"—asks Cardinal Newman in his memorable essay upon the *Catholicity of the Anglican Church* in the *British Critic* of January, 1840,—" has it been moving through three hundred years? Where does it find itself at the end? Lutherans have tended to Rationalism; Calvinists have become Socinians; but what has it become? As far as its formularies are concerned, it may be said all along to have grown towards a more perfect Catholicism than that with which it started at the time of its estrangement; every act, every crisis which marks its course has been upward. It never was in so miserable case as in the reigns of Edward and Elizabeth. At the end of Elizabeth's there was a conspicuous revival of the true doctrine. Advancements were made in the Canons of 1603. How much was done under Charles I. need not be said; and done permanently, so as to remain to this day, in spite of the storm which immediately arose, sweeping off the chief agents in the work, and for a time levelling the Church to the ground. More was done than even yet appears, as a philosophical writer has lately remarked, in the Convocation of 1661."[1]

Pregnant words indeed of prophetic import; particularly when we consider the progress of the Church of God in this land since the above words were written nearly fifty years ago :—How "the desolations of many generations" have been built up";[2] how the supernatural life of the Church, both severally in her members and collectively in her organic union with the whole Body of Christ, has been deepened and developed by the Divinely ordained "joints and bands" of the Apostolic ministry and Sacraments[3]; how this life which is Catholic as well as supernatural—the life, that is, of "the Spirit of the Lord [Who] filleth the world"[4] in quickening and sanctifying the one only Church of God—has been increasingly manifested in the Note of Holiness, perpetuating the Life of God Incarnate upon earth; in the clearer apprehension and systematic teaching of dogmatic truth; in the restored solemnities of Catholic worship; and in renewed missionary effort both at home and abroad. All this, and more, is clear to those who have eyes to see and unprejudiced minds to understand the events and signs of the present time.

[1] *Cf. Essays Critical and Historical*, Fifth Edition, vol. II. p. 55 (London, 1881).
[2] Isai. lxi. 4. [3] Col. ii. 19. [4] Wisdom i. 7.

The roots of this wonderful revival which has marked Church life in England during the reign of her most gracious Majesty Queen Victoria are deeply embedded in our national history; the Bishops and orthodox Clergy of the Restoration period faithfully did their part in preparing for it; in that they strengthened the things which remained, that were then ready to perish,[1] by re-affirming fundamental principles of faith and discipline; and thus consolidated what has since become the established Order of this Church and Realm. Their firmness in maintaining the Catholic Faith in its integrity, as set forth in the three Creeds, combined with their moderation in not then enforcing the observance of the ancient ceremonial, at the same time that they were careful to prepare the ground for its restoration in the order of God's providence, have borne fruit, after the lapse of two hundred years, in that work of restoration which may serve to indicate how much "more was done than even yet appears in the Convocation of 1661." May we not be encouraged by God's merciful loving kindness towards His Church in this land in hoping that the attraction of the Sacramental Presence of His Incarnate Son, continually sanctifying our Altars and hallowing our Churches, in perpetually waiting upon the spiritual needs of the children of men, may be one of the blessings still in store, bequeathed to us and

---

[1] Rev. iii. 2.

rendered available by the fidelity and Catholic temper of the Caroline Divines, who firmly took their stand *super antiquas vias*?

Can we then suppose that the Revisers of 1661, as theologians and honest men, if they had really intended thus to depart from all antiquity in disallowing the practice of Reservation, then confessedly permitted (see Chap. II. p. 14), though commonly disused, would have adopted the crooked policy of forbidding it by a side-wind, without a single hint as to any such intention, under the pretext of "the procuring of reverence" or "for the better direction for them that are to officiate"? But even granting, for the sake of argument, such an unreasonable hypothesis, can we conceive it possible that Bishop Cosin, who probably penned this rubric and certainly revised it, would so completely have stultified himself as thus to forbid one of the ceremonial usages retained in 1549, which he had himself justified as being "since omitted only, and not condemned" (see Chap. III. pp. 23—25); and in so doing to ground his prohibition upon the old canonical rule still possessing statutory authority (as he himself testifies) which enjoins and regulates the very practice which this rubric is now supposed to forbid?

It is further to be observed that this direction (in the Constitution) to renew the Sacrament every Sunday at the least, combined with the provision that "if any remain of that which was consecrated, the Priest and his ministers shall eat and consume the same," clearly indicates that the similar direction in our present rubric is not inconsistent with the Reservation of that which is newly consecrated, provided that "if any remain of that which was consecrated" the previous Sunday, "it shall not be carried out of the Church, but the Priest and such other of the Communicants as he shall then call unto him shall immediately after the Blessing reverently eat and drink the same"; also that the clause "if any remain" does not refer to that which, being newly consecrated, may (according to the canonical usage of the Church of England) be reserved "*ad opus morientium*," but to that which may be left from the previous Sunday, and thus be no longer required.

Hence it is manifest that the First-part of this Constitution, when examined in its historical, legal, and liturgical bearings, throws a flood of light upon the Sixth Post-communion rubric, which, so far from forbidding Reservation, is thus seen to pre-suppose (wherever practicable) the primitive custom of reserving "so much of the Sacrament of the Body and Blood" as may serve for the Communion of the sick.[1]

We must not omit to notice that this usage is enjoined as a precept, and may not therefore be wilfully neglected without sin; moreover, resting as

---

[1] *Cf. The Communion of the Sick*, Prayer Book of 1549.

it does upon ecclesiastical and statutory authority, it is included *de facto* in the Order of "this Church and Realm," which all Priests at their Ordination have solemnly promised to observe "by the help of the Lord."

3. We will now proceed to the consideration of the Second-part of this Constitution, which enjoins that the Eucharist be carried to the sick with due reverence on the part of priest and people. This injunction of Archbishop Peccham, who in his day was distinguished by his diligence in the maintenance of Church discipline and the reforming of abuses throughout the province of Canterbury, really dates from A.D. 1279, or the seventh year of Edward the First; it is therefore two years anterior to that part of the Provincial Constitution which we have already been considering; but inasmuch as it deals with the method in which the holy Sacrament is to be ministered to the sick, just as the Constitution of 1281 enjoins the manner in which the Eucharist is to be reserved in every parish church, it is regarded by Lyndwood as virtually part of the same Constitution, and thus is placed after it both by that learned Canonist and also by Bishop Gibson.[1]

Here it is worthy of notice that the custom of reserving the Sacrament of the Eucharist in the

---

[1] *Cf. Provinciale*, pp. 248, 249. *Codex Juris Eccles. Anglicani*, vol. I. pp. 264, 284.

Church for the Communion of the Sick and Dying, as part of the *Jus Commune Ecclesiasticum*, was observed (as we have already seen) long before the time of Archbishop Peccham; all therefore that was done by this vigilant Primate, in this Constitution of the province of Canterbury, was to support and regulate this primitive tradition by means of the provisions and injunctions of Canon Law. The fact also that the former part of the Constitution, which regulates the custom of reserving the Eucharist in church, was in point of time subsequent to that which ordains that it be carried to the sick with due reverence, affords additional evidence (if indeed such were needed) that the primary intention of the Church in such reservation is to provide for the needs of the sick and dying, or, as Lyndwood says, *ad opus morientium*.

The second part of this Constitution is as follows:—

"Statuimus, ut Sacramentum Eucharistiæ circumferatur cum debita reverentia ad ægrotos, Sacerdote saltem induto Superpellicio, gerente Orarium cum lumine prævio in lucerna cum Campana, ut populus ad reverentiam debitam excitetur; qui ad prosternendum se, vel adorandum saltem humiliter, informetur Sacerdotali prudentia, ubicunque Regem Gloriæ sub panis latibulo evenerit deportari; et de hoc Archidiaconi in suorum remissionem peccaminum sint sollictiti. Et quos circa hoc negligentes invenerint, disciplina rigida castigent."[1]

Thus it is ordained by the Ecclesiastical Law of

[1] *Cf.* Lyndwood's *Provinciale*, lib. III. tit. 26, pp. 249, 250. Bishop Gibson's *Codex*, vol. I. p. 484.

Enjoined by the Ecclesiastical Law. 95

England that the Sacrament of the Eucharist is to be carried to the sick with due reverence; the Priest at least[1] being habited in a Surplice and wearing a Stole,[2] having a light carried before in a lantern[3] with a bell, that the people may be summoned to shew such respect as is fitting, either in kneeling[4] or at least in humbly bowing down, as

[1] Thus, as Lyndwood observes, although a surplice may be dispensed with on the part of the minister who accompanies the priest in this ministration, nevertheless it is more fitting that even the priest's minister (or clerk) should be habited in a surplice, regard being had to the nature of the benefice and the means of the same.

[2] Here Lyndwood, who is quoted by Bishop Gibson, is careful to note that the priest (*Sacerdos*), *i.e.* the officiating priest (*Executor Officii* in the Sarum and York rubrics), ought always to wear his stole in divine service:—"*Orarium, i.e. Stolam, qua Sacerdos in omni obsequio Divino uti debet, et suo collo imponitur ut significet se jugum Domini suscepisse.*"

[3] This is ordered, according to Lyndwood, in order to signify that Christ is the brightness of eternal light, "*candor Lucis æternæ,*" as he had before said in commenting upon the Constitution of Archbishop Walter, which enjoins the use of the two Altar-lights at the time of Celebration:—"*Candela namque sic ardens significat Ipsum Christum, qui est splendor Lucis æternæ*" (*vide supra*, p. 22). The use of the lantern is obviously a matter of practical convenience to protect the light from wind and rain.

[4] *Ad prosternendum se* is the expression used in the original, which Lyndwood explains as "*genua ad terram flectendo.*" *Adorandum*, enjoined as an alternative act of reverence, he explains as—"*Cum inclinatione capitis, et cordis devotione, et manum expansione, sive etiam elevatione, cum Orationis devotæ vocali expressione, ut scilicet sic dicatur:*—'Salve, Lux mundi! Verbum Patris, Hostia vera; Viva Caro, Deitas integra, verus Homo':—

'Salve, Caro Christi, quæ pro me passa fuisti.
Intus me munda, Christi Caro, Sanguis et unda.

'*Et consimili modo dicatur in elevatione Corporis Christi in Missa.
. . . . Ego tamen soleo sic dicere:*—

instructed beforehand by their pastor, wheresoever the King of Glory[1] may be carried in His holy Sacrament;[2] moreover, that the Archdeacons[3] are to be careful in putting an end to their own omissions herein, and in correcting with strict discipline[4] those whom they shall find negligent in this matter.

Bishop Gibson reminds us that Lyndwood's gloss upon this Constitution, whereof the greater part (which more nearly concerns ourselves) is here given in the notes by way of commentary, as in the *Provinciale*, is of great authority, as witnessing to the traditional practice of the Church of England; consequently the rules here laid down have become in effect part of the Common Law of the Church. It is not indeed contended that the directions here prescribed should, under altered circumstances, be

> 'Ave, verum Corpus, natum ex Maria Virgine!
> Vere passum, immolatum in Cruce pro nomine!
> Cujus latus vulneratum, vero fluxit sanguine;
> Esto nobis prægustatum, mortis in examine.
> O dulcis, O pie, O Jesu, fili Mariæ.' "

Humiliter is noted as—" *Cum inclinatione capitis, et prædixi, oculisque in terram demissis.*"

[1] The King of Glory, i.e. "*Ipsum Christum secundum Humanitatem glorificatam.*"

[2] In His holy Sacrament; literally *sub panis latibulo*, i.e. "*Specie sive occultatione.*"—Under the sacramental species or forms of Bread and Wine.

[3] *Archidiaconi.* Lyndwood adds—"*et alii Visitantes.*" Thus all ordinaries are bound by the Ecclesiastical Law to take order for the due observance of this Constitution.

[4] *Disciplina rigida;* i.e. *Aspera vel austera. Debet tamen talis rigiditas temperari mansuetudine.* Therefore discipline is to be enforced with moderation.

observed in detail; but that they should be regarded as setting forth the standard to be aimed at in this ministration, and as indicating that spirit of devotion and external reverence by which our Catholic forefathers manifested their faith in the reality of Christ's presence in His holy Mysteries; which, in honour of so great a Sacrament, are due from us their children in the same historic communion of the Church in this land.

From Lyndwood's comments upon this Constitution it is evident that considerable latitude and freedom were allowed in the manner of observing the directions it enjoins. For instance, it is ordered that the priest carry the Sacrament before his breast,[1]

[1] The Latin rubrics and commentaries respecting the Administration of the Holy Communion direct (either explicitly or by implication) that the priest is to carry the Eucharist *before his breast;* thus Lyndwood upon this Constitution:—"*quod Sacerdos Eucharistiam reverenter gerat ante pectus suum*"; and the *Rituale Romanum:*—"*ante pectus cum omni reverentia et timore*"; also a Belgian Commentary of the 17th century, *Directorium Sacerdotale,* printed at Louvain, has these golden words, which should be kept in mind by all who minister in holy things :—"*Caveat autem Celebrans cum hæc dicit ne per templum oculis vagetur, sed oculis demissis Sacramentum respiciat, verbis factisque ita se gerat ut devotio adstantium excitetur, non præcipitanter Sacramentum distribuat, cauteque se gerat ne ex pyxide vel manu aliquid, cadat.*" Hence the practice of carrying the Sacrament above the head, adopted by some clergy in administering the Holy Communion, is contrary to the Church's traditional custom, which is based upon grounds of reverence, convenience, and propriety. Therefore any ceremonial observance which is irreverent, inconvenient, or grotesque may be regarded as the expression of some personal idiosyncracy, or as indicating an imperfect acquaintance with the due Order of the Church. If the author may venture to offer a suggestion to his brethren, he would say that two things are imperatively needed by the

and that the tabernacle or pyx[1] in which it is conveyed to the sick be covered with a fair and decent veil.[2] From which it is evident that the light here

English clergy, viz.—more accurate knowledge concerning the *principles* of Divine Service, and the spirit of *recollection* in all their ministrations.

[1] According to Lyndwood (*Provinciale*, p. 248, n. *g*), the expense of providing a suitable tabernacle devolves upon the curate, while the pyx is to be provided by the parish; as in the Register of Walter Gray, Archbishop of York, some thirty years anterior to the Constitution of Archbishop Peccham, in which we find the pyx included among the Church ornaments to be provided by the parishioners (*vide supra*, p. 23). Among the sacred vessels at St. Oswald's, Durham, there is a beautiful ciborium or covered chalice of silver gilt, dating from the end of the 17th century, which during the incumbency of the late Dr. Dykes, who will always be revered as the saintly and devoted Vicar of St. Oswald's, was used for reserving the Blessed Sacrament for the sick. Such *ciboria* are not uncommon among the sacred vessels provided in the 16th and 17th centuries; for the most part no doubt they were intended to serve as chalices in the Administration of Holy Communion, but considering that the modern theory, which assumes that Reservation is now forbidden by the sixth Post-communion rubric, had not then been heard of, it is probable that they were so fashioned in order to serve the additional purpose of reserving the Eucharist for the sick. It is to be remembered that both the tabernacle and pyx are statutable ornaments in virtue of 25 Hen. VIII., which, having been in use "in this Church of England by the authority of Parliament in the second year of the reign of King Edward the Sixth," are therefore enjoined still. (*Cf.* Chapter III. 1.)

[2] *Et quod Tabernaculum, in quo portatur, operiatur mundo velamine.* Here we find additional evidence of the liturgical usage of veiling the reserved Sacrament, enjoined by the compilers of the Scotch Office of 1637, and the revisers of our English Office in 1661; who inserted the present rubric, directing that "what remaineth of the consecrated Elements," when reserved upon the Lord's Table, shall be covered "with a fair linen cloth." An injunction which shews that they advisedly recognised the *principle* of Reservation, in thus prescribing a ceremonial observance traditionally attendant thereon; and one moreover which significantly indicates that reverence, due to the holy Mysteries *extra usum Sacramenti*, which we learn from their

mentioned is to be carried by the minister; for the light ought to go before, as here enjoined. But if in case of necessity it happened that the priest had no minister at hand to bear the accustomed light, it is suggested that he may suspend the lantern on his arm and manage the bell as best he can; as is the wont (observes Lyndwood) of country parsons in wide parishes when carrying the Viaticum to sick persons in remote districts; who, whenever they proceed on horse-back, affix the lantern and bell to their horse's head-gear, and in this are not to be reprehended, because necessity has no law.[1]

writings (*vid. sup.* pp. 29—31). Here also it is important to note that this rubric, so far from being without liturgical precedent, as some persons apparently imagine, witnesses to the antiquity of the custom of reverently veiling the reserved Sacrament, a usage which, as we have already seen (*Cf.* Chapter III. 3), was observed in the earlier ages of the Church, and is still ordered in the present Roman rite whenever the Eucharist is reserved until the end of Mass. It is therefore to be regretted that in some places clergy have innovated upon the established Order of the Church, either by receiving "what remaineth of the consecrated Elements" *before* the Post-Communion, thereby obscuring the witness of this rubric to the *principle* of Reservation, or (which is of much less consequence) by neglecting to cover the reserved Eucharist with a fair linen veil (*mundo velamine*), as directed both in the *Provinciale* and also in this rubric. *A little knowledge* is proverbially dangerous; so in this matter more accurate acquaintance with the *Origines Liturgicæ*, both of the Anglican and Latin rites, would have revealed the substantial agreement which in this respect subsists between the *Missale Romanum* and the *Book of Common Prayer*. Until such knowledge is acquired it is surely not out of place to suggest that it would be presumptuous to depart from the customs of our fathers, and to commend to any who may be unadvisedly disposed to do so the epigrammatic saying of the late Master of Trinity:—" *We are none of us infallible, no, not even the youngest of us.*"

[1] *Provinciale*, p. 249, note (x).

It is probable that for the present it will, for the most part, be found desirable to recur to the custom of the Church in primitive times; by carrying the Holy Sacrament to the sick without needlessly attracting the attention of those who are out of sympathy with her spirit, and unfamiliar with the traditional observances, which are part of our undoubted heritage in the Communion "of the whole Catholic Church of Christ." Indeed, there can be no doubt that in this manner Reservation is unobtrusively but widely practised, and that with no lack of reverence, at the present time.

Twenty years ago it was the writer's privilege thus to administer the Holy Communion with the reserved Sacrament, on repeated occasions, to his most revered friend and brother, the late Dr. Dykes of Durham, with whom he was then associated as Assistant Curate of St. Oswald's. Ten or twelve years earlier, when he was yet a student at the University, he remembers that this custom was observed in a Yorkshire parish where he was periodically resident in vacation time.

In the previous generation, as he has been credibly informed, the Eucharist was carried from the Altar of Durham Cathedral for the Communion of sick persons in the "College," or Cathedral Close.[1] Indeed, it is said that the practice of

---

[1] The author is aware that the accuracy of this statement, which has already been made public, has been questioned; but he has recently

Reservation, like other Catholic usages, has been traditional at Durham, which would seem to indicate that the clergy of the Caroline period had no suspicion that this primitive custom was forbidden by the then recent revision of the *Book of Common Prayer*.

Such therefore is the canonical rule of the Church

---

been assured by those who have long been connected with Durham Cathedral that there is "no doubt that it was so, but that probably there is no one now living who is old enough to give evidence about the time previous to 1849." The author has also been informed by one of the most respected of the Yorkshire clergy that fifty years ago Durham Cathedral was very remarkable in the reverent order and dignity of its services, and in the traditional observance of Catholic usages. Some twenty years ago another Yorkshire Incumbent, who was at Durham School in the early part of this century, assured the Rev. George Ornsby, then Vicar of Fishlake, "that he had the most distinct remembrance of the altar-candles being then lighted at the Cathedral every Sunday *morning*, in anticipation of the Celebration of Holy Communion." *Cf. Bp. Cosin's Correspondence*, vol. i. xxvii. note, edited by the late Rev. George Ornsby (Surtees Society, 1869). A friend who served his title about forty years ago writes:—"I remember, in my old curacy in Derbyshire, hearing that the Sacrament had been carried from the Church through the village to the sick; and I have no doubt this tradition remains in many villages.

"The custom must have remained and have been handed down from the time of the first Prayer Book (which carried on the old tradition), when reservation was enjoined by the first rubric of the Order for the Communion of the Sick.

"I take it that we are all at liberty to do this, as nothing is 'ungodly' in the first Book, which is spoken of in the Act of Uniformity, authorising the second Book, as 'a very godly Order, etc., agreeable to the Word of God and the Primitive Church.'

"I have frequently carried the Sacrament from the early Celebration to the sick."

Another friend "confirms" the accuracy of the author's statement respecting the custom of Reservation at Durham.

of England, set forth in the Constitution of Archbishop Peccham (which we have been considering) still standing unrepealed among the Constitutions of the Province of Canterbury; which authorises the Reservation of the Blessed Sacrament for the Communion of the sick and dying, and which is found, upon historical, legal, and liturgical investigation, to be in no wise inconsistent with the Order prescribed in the later formularies of the Church.

Nothing can be alleged as repealing the foregoing Constitution which, in virtue of 25 Hen. VIII., has the force of Statute Law, save the sixth Post-communion rubric, which likewise possesses statutory authority under the Act of Uniformity of 1662. But we have already shewn that this rubric was inserted by the Catholic prelates and divines of the Caroline era with a totally different purpose, viz. as the traditional safeguard against the profanation of Christ's holy Mysteries, and as carrying on the old canonical provision for the reverent consumption of the consecrated Elements, which might not be required for purposes of Communion.[1] Moreover, it

---

[1] Upon carefully collating the sixth Post-communion rubric and the previous rubric, which directs the priest reverently to place upon the Lord's Table "what remaineth of the consecrated Elements, covering the same with a fine linen cloth"—with the analogous usages referred to by S. Gelasius, Amalarius, and Micrologus in the earlier ages of the Church, and subsequently by Durandus and Lyndwood—it will be found that these rubrics, when regarded in the light of Catholic antiquity, direct the priest, according to the present English rite, in the first place to reserve the Blessed Sacrament at every Celebration; obviously,

must be remembered that no evidence has hitherto been adduced in support of the theory that this rubric carries with it any prohibition of the primitive and Catholic tradition of reserving the Eucharist for the sick; and further, that modern commentaries, in which this theory is adopted, are in this respect based upon a mere assumption, which the history of this rubric proves to be untenable. Further, that neither Laud nor Wren, who in the first instance penned this rubric, nor Cosin who revised it, nor the bishops and clergy of both Convocations who adopted it, give so much as a hint that it was intended to prohibit, or in any degree to affect, the traditional usage of the Church in reserving the holy Mysteries; but on the contrary, that the great Caroline divines, as we learn from their writings and the history of their lives, were deeply impressed by

---

therefore, it cannot be supposed that the latter rubric virtually forbids what the former explicitly enjoins. In the next place, upon ordinary occasions he "shall immediately after the Blessing reverently eat and drink the same." But every Sunday at the least, as directed by the Ecclesiastical Law, the priest is to reserve so much as he shall think sufficient for the Communion of the Sick in the week following, placing the Eucharist thus reserved in a comely pyx within the tabernacle (according to the Provincial Constitution); and then "with his ministers" (if need be), according to St. Gelasius and the Commentary of Lyndwood, or, in case they have not then communicated, with "such other of the communicants as he shall then call unto him," shall receive and consume any that may no longer be required for purposes of Communion, whether remaining from the previous Sunday or at that particular Celebration. "*Et Hostias*," says Lyndwood, "*si quæ fuerint remanentes, a Sacerdote et ejus Ministris, videlicet Diacono et Subdiacono, recipi et consumi.*"

the duty of handing on unimpaired to their successors that deposit of faith, together with that Order of worship and discipline, which they had themselves received.

If it be objected that it is incredible that the practice of Reservation can be intended by the Church, notwithstanding the entire absence of explicit directions in her Offices, the obvious reply is that there never were any such explicit directions in the ancient Service Books of the Church of England; and that the difficulty which suggests this objection results in the first place from lack of acquaintance with the earlier formularies and customs of the Church, and in the second, from the too common though illogical habit of mind which regards the mediæval Church of England from a modern Roman standpoint. Such directions are to be found in the *Rituale Romanum*, and subordinately in the Roman Missal, it is true; but they are conspicuous by their absence in the mediæval Service Books of the Church of England.[1] In fact,

---

[1] The following is the Order for the Communion of the Sick from the *York Manual*, which is almost identical with that in the *Sarum Manual*:—

Facta Unctione totaliter, expediens est ut Sacerdos ante Communionem inquirat ab infirmo an aliqua alia peccata sibi ad memoriam occurrant, de quibus non erat confessus. Nam posset esse quod aut per devotas orationes Sacerdotis sive aliorum Deus cor infirmi illustraret, et daret ei gratiam verius et plenius confiteri. Et postea interroget eum Sacerdos si recognoscat Corpus et Sanguinem Domini nostri Jesu Christi, sic dicendo:—

Frater, credis quod sacramentum quod tractatur in altari sub forma panis est verum Corpus et Sanguis Domini nostri Jesu Christi—*Respondeat infirmus dicens:* Credo.

Deinde communicetur infirmus, nisi prius communicatus fuerit, et nisi de

the primitive custom of reserving the Eucharist for
the Sick rested exclusively, within the canonical

*vomitu vel alia irreverentia probabiliter timeatur : in quo casu Sacerdos dicat
infirmo sic :—*
Frater, in hoc casu sufficit tibi vera fides et bona voluntas; tantum Crede
et manducasti.
Isti non debent sumere Corpus Christi.
  Dum vomit infirmus non debet sumere Corpus
  Christi: nisi credit ; credendo fideliter egit.
  Ebrius, insanus, erroneus, et male credens,
  Et pueri ; Corpus Christi non suscipiant hi.
  Non nisi mense semel aliquis communicet æger.
Et nota, quod Sacerdos infirmus et communicandus induetur stola.

Hic communicetur infirmus, Sacerdote dicente hoc modo:
Corpus Domini nostri Jesu Christi custodiat corpus tuum et animam
tuam in vitam æternam. Amen.

*Deinde dicat Sacerdos, sine Dominus vobiscum sed tantum cum Oremus,
orationem sequentem, quod non dicitur nisi tantum quando infirmus communicetur. Oratio.*

Domine, sancte Pater, omnipotens æterne Deus, Te fideliter deprecamur
ut huic fratri nostro *N.*, accipienti sacrosanctum Corpus et Sanguinem Jesu
Christi, Filii Tui, Domini nostri, tam corporis quam animæ sit salus per
eundem Christum Dominum nostrum.

*   *   *   *   *   *

*Si Episcopus adest, absolvat infirmum et dicat has orationes. Sin autem,
Sacerdos hæc compleat. Oratio.*

Dominus Jesus Christus apud te sit, ut te defendat; intra te sit, ut te
reficiat; circa te sit, ut te conservet; ante te sit, ut te deducat; post te sit,
ut te justificet; super te sit, ut te benedicat. Qui cum Patre et Spiritu
Sancto vivit et regnat Deus per omnia sæcula sæculorum. Amen.

Cf. The York Manual, pp. 51, 52, 53, and 50*, 51* (Surtees Society, 1874). Very beautiful Benedictions follow, which, with the above prayer, appear to have suggested the similar prayer and benediction in the present English Order for the Visitation of the Sick. There is no doubt that in mediæval times the sick were commonly communicated with the reserved Sacrament, but at the same time Mass for the sick was also provided, with collect, epistle, and gospel, as in the *Book of Common Prayer*. Bishop Cosin thus comments upon the Collect at the Communion of the Sick :—" *In ord. Sarum similis oratio habetur ad Missam pro infirmo morti proximo.*" (*Cf. Notes on the Common Prayer*, p. 370.) We have already seen (*vid. sup.* p. 17, note) that in the earlier ages of the Church the private Celebration for the Sick went on concurrently with the custom of Reservation; probably this custom, of which we have a survival in the Latin *Missa pro infirmis*, continued to be observed in mediæval times, particularly in houses with jurisdiction of the Bishops of England, upon the immemorial tradition of the Church, subsequently private chapels or oratories, and so gave rise to our present Order, in which it is specially provided, with a view to celebration, that there is to be "*a convenient place in the sick man's house, with all things so prepared, that the curate may reverently minister.*" Nothing is prescribed in the Sarum and York Manuals as to Celebration or Reservation, so the Order therein given might be used in either case; thus both were provided for in the Prayer Book of 1549. The rubrics directing Reservation were omitted in 1552, but restored in the Latin Book of 1560; in 1661 the rubrics referring to Celebration were made more explicit and re-cast after the fashion of 1549, but there was no substantial alteration. Consequently the custom of Reservation, so far as it is affected by the rubrics, remains exactly where it was before, in the words of Bishop Cosin, as "omitted only, but not condemned" (*vid. sup.* p. 24). Therefore it is not surprising to find Bishop Sparrow, who was also one of the Revisers in 1661, advocating the practice of Reservation as enjoined in 1549, notwithstanding the absence of any rubric to that effect in the English Prayer Book since 1552. It is sometimes urged that the explicit directions of 1661 virtually exclude the custom of Reservation, which, it is admitted, may have been permissible before; but the answer is that, although the rubric was defective in not directing how much of the public Office should be used for the Communion of the Sick, an omission which was corrected in 1661, the Order then, as now, had reference primarily to the case of private *Celebration*; this is evident from the following rubric in the Order for *The Celebration of the Holy Communion for the Sick* in 1549 :—*At the time of the distribution of the Holy Sacrament, the Priest shall first receive the Communion himself, etc.*, which has been continued ever since. At the same time we have concurrent testimony to the tradition of Reservation for the Sick,—positively in the Latin Prayer Book of 1560, and negatively in the fact that no direction is given in our present Order as to the method to be adopted in case there be a Celebration in Church upon the same day whereon the sick is to be communicated; consequently we are of necessity referred, as suggested by one of the Revisers in 1661, to the "former directions in times past" (*Cf. Rationale* by Bp. of *Exon.*, London, 1668, p. 349). Moreover, in old times Reservation for the Sick did not rest upon rubrical directions, but upon primitive tradition and canonical sanction; so likewise with ourselves.

enjoined and regulated (as we have already seen) by the enactments and commentaries of Canon and Common Law.

Here then we have a remarkable example of the concordance which subsists between the established Order of this Church and Realm, as set forth in the *Book of Common Prayer*, illustrated and supported by the Ecclesiastical Law, and the venerable monuments of Catholic antiquity.

CHAPTER V.

OF COMMUNION UNDER BOTH KINDS.

IN treating of the Reservation of the Blessed Sacrament, the further question of Communion under both kinds ought not to be passed over in silence; although the controversy which has gathered round it suggests the need of dispassionate consideration in dealing with this important subject in its theological, historical, and practical bearings.

1. In the first place it must be remembered that by an unbroken and universal tradition, extending down to well-nigh the thirteenth century of the Christian era, the Holy Communion was uniformly administered in the Church *under both kinds*, according to the sacred Institution of Jesus Christ our Lord. Thus, in conformity with the normal and divinely ordained rule of the Christian Church, "the Cup of Blessing," which, as S. Paul teaches, "is the Communion of the Blood of Christ," was administered to the faithful in the public Liturgy, together with that hallowed Bread which, as the same Apostle testifies, is "the Communion of the Body of Christ,"[1] for nearly twelve hundred years.

[1] 1 Cor. x. 16.

In fact, the public administration of Holy Communion under both kinds rests upon the threefold basis of the Divine Institution, the Common Law of the Church, as witnessed by the universal custom of Christendom, and the explicit directions and provisions of the Canon Law, both in primitive and early mediæval times. Hence the later practice of administering Communion exclusively in one kind is not only barred by the Divine command—"*Drink ye all of it*"—which is equally binding upon all Christians, priests and laity alike, with the parallel command,—"*Take, eat; this is My Body.*"[1] But, as we have already seen, with regard to the usage of Reservation, *the Common Law of the Church can only be abrogated by the custom of the whole Church* (*vide supra*, pp. 72—75).

If, therefore, it would be *ultra vires* on the part of the Church of England to forbid such Catholic usages as the primitive custom of reserving the Eucharist and the observance of the traditional ceremonial in celebrating the holy Mysteries, which, though probably of Apostolic origin, rest mainly upon the Common Law of the Church, subsequently regulated by the Canon Law; much less is it within the competence of any particular Church, such as the Church of the Roman patriarchate, to abrogate the custom of the universal Church, and in this respect to depart not only from all antiquity, but from the

[1] S. Matt. xxvi. 26, 27.

living practice of the rest of Christendom in the ancient patriarchates of Jerusalem, Antioch, Alexandria, and Constantinople; restored, after the lapse of three hundred years, in the distinct province of the Isles of Britain, and thence handed on to the great continent of America and to the world-wide dependencies of our Colonial Empire. For it must be remembered that the Catholic tradition of Communion in both kinds, still observed in so large a portion of the Christian world, rests primarily upon the Divine Institution of the Eucharistic Mystery; and therefore the attempt to abrogate it involves the reversal of a Divine command by virtually substituting for the Lord's words—"DRINK YE ALL OF IT"—the prohibition, *Drink ye none of it under pain of excommunication.*

We have already seen (*Cf.* p. 36) that Pope Gelasius interdicts the refusal of the chalice no less explicitly than his successors in later times have interdicted its administration. His decree is recorded by Gratian in his *Decretum,* as incorporated in the Canon Law of Western Christendom, where it stands to this present day, as an abiding witness to the fidelity of the Roman Church in primitive times to the Divine command (illustrated by the uniform tradition of the whole Church) in her public administration of the holy Mysteries of the Lord's Body and Blood. Thus the later practice of the Roman Church unhappily ignores her ancient discipline, enforced under pain of spiritual censure both by S. Gelasius and by his predecessors, Pope Julius and the great S. Leo. "We have learned," says Pope Gelasius in his decree, "that certain persons, having received only the Sacrament of the Lord's Body, abstain from the Chalice of His Blood; which persons (who are bound, as is reported, by I know not what superstition) should without doubt either partake of the Sacraments in their entirety, or be excluded from the entire Sacraments, BECAUSE THE DIVISION OF ONE AND THE SAME MYSTERY CANNOT TAKE PLACE WITHOUT GREAT SACRILEGE."

Before him, Pope Leo the Great, about the year 444, had excommunicated certain Manichæan heretics, who (holding the use of wine to be unlawful) objected to the Sacramental Cup;[1] while Pope Julius, who presided over the Roman Church from A.D. 336 to 352, altogether forbids the public administration of the Eucharist even by *intinction*; and enjoins that the Bread and the Cup are to be

[1] *Cf.* Bp. Forbes, *Explanation of the Thirty-nine Articles,—De utraque Specie*, p. 597. It is to be observed that the learned Canonist, Van Espen, who does not cite the above decree in his Summary of Gratian's *Decretum*, under the impression, apparently, that its authenticity was doubtful, has omitted to notice that it is also recorded by Micrologus, who flourished some two hundred and fifty years before Gratian compiled his *Decretum*, or *Corpus Juris Canonici*, about the year 1051; and that it is evidently regarded as both genuine and authentic by this earlier writer in his treatise, *De Missa rite Celebranda*, before referred to (see pp. 33 and 36). Its authenticity, therefore, does not rest solely upon the authority of Gratian; *Decretum*, pars III. *De Consecratione*, Distinctio II. 12, *Comperimus*.

received separately, according to the Lord's Institution:—"*et seorsum panem, et seorsum calicem, juxta Dominicam institutionem, sumenda docet.*"[1]

At the same time the Divine gift was held to be wholly conveyed "through every portion of either element"; as S. Cyril of Alexandria, cited by Archdeacon Wilberforce in his invaluable work on the *Doctrine of the Holy Eucharist*, teaches in the following comment on S. John vi. 57:—

"For as S. Paul says, 'a little leaven leaveneth the whole lump,' so the very smallest portion of the Eucharist (ὀλιγίστη εὐλογία) transfuses our whole body into itself, and fills us with its own energy; and thus Christ comes to exist in us, and we in Him."[2]

Again, this doctrine has evidently suggested certain significant expressions which are found both in the Ambrosian and other ancient liturgies:—

"Singuli accipiunt Christum Dominum, et in singulis portionibus totus est; nec per singulos minuitur, sed integrum se præbet in singulis."[3]

Also in the English Liturgy of 1549, which, in the following passage from one of the general rubrics, as in other respects, so strikingly illustrates the mind and purpose of the Fathers and the liturgical practice of antiquity:—

"And men must not think less to be received in part than in

---

[1] Micrologus, *De Missa rite Celebranda*, cap. xix.

[2] *Cf. The Doctrine of the Holy Eucharist*, by the late Archdeacon Wilberforce, Second Edition, p. 70 (London, 1853).

[3] *Ibid.* p. 71, cited from Muratori, *De Rebus Liturgicis*, i. p. 126.

the whole, but in each of them the whole body of our Saviour Jesu Christ":

as though these words had been suggested by the above expression in the Ambrosian rite,—*in singulis portionibus totus est.*

This doctrine is likewise taught by S. Cæsarius, bishop of Arles in the fifth century, when comparing the bestowal of the Divine Gift in the Eucharist with the distribution of manna :—

"The sacred perception of the Eucharist does not depend upon its quantity, but upon its efficacy. This Body, when the priest distributes it, is as much in the smallest portion as in the whole. When the congregation of the faithful receive it, as it is fully in all of them, so it is perfectly in each. We may apply to it the Apostle's words :—' He that hath much shall have nothing over; he that hath little shall have no lack.' If we gave the hungry bread to eat, each one severally would not receive that which was bestowed upon the whole, but each must take his own separate portion for himself. But, when *this Bread* is taken, each one severally receives not less than the collective body. One receives the whole, two receive it, many receive it, without any diminution; because the blessing of this Sacrament is susceptible of being distributed, but it is not susceptible of being exhausted by distribution."[1]

It is only fair to add that the authors of the above quotations, which indicate the completeness of the Gift in the smallest portion of the Eucharist, were all in the habit of administering and receiving the holy Mysteries under both kinds; their writings therefore can only apply subordinately to exceptional

[1] Cæsarii Homilia, vii. *Bib. Patrum Max.* VIII. p. 825, cited by Archdeacon Wilberforce.

8

administration in either kind; while the words of S. Gelasius would lead to the conclusion that this holy Father, who presided over the Roman Church in the latter part of the fifth century, taught explicitly that no such division of one and the same mystery could be permitted without great sacrilege. On the other hand, it must be remembered that the above passages have reference to the public administration of the Eucharist, and consequently do not strictly apply to the exceptional circumstances of private ministrations. They therefore may be regarded as shewing that inasmuch as the Divine Gift is bestowed in its fulness in the very smallest portion of the consecrated Elements, so the mind of the Church is not averse to the practice of administering the Communion in either kind in cases of necessity.

We must, however, guard against the erroneous conclusion that, because the sacramental Gift is fully bestowed under either species, its *effect* is the same as though communicated under both kinds. Our Lord graciously gives Himself to us in the Eucharistic Mystery under the form of food; and we must remember that, inasmuch as the Sacraments cause what they signify, the effects of our Lord's presence will be diverse under the diverse kinds of food which He has consecrated to be the *media* whereby He gives Himself to us in all the fulness of His grace; in short, that in the supernatural order these effects will be analogous to those of the means employed in the natural order; as the Church teaches in the Catechism that "the benefits whereof we are partakers thereby" are "the strengthening and refreshing of our souls by the Body and Blood of Christ, *as our bodies are by the bread and wine.*" And so, theologians have held that the Communion under each kind is effectual to that end whereunto it has been ordained by Christ Himself, and that this end is attained by the devout receiving of the means ordained, and (ordinarily) not otherwise. Hence it follows that, in the Holy Communion of the Lord's Body and Blood, while Christ gives Himself wholly to us under the form of Bread to sustain our supernatural life and to endue us with ghostly strength, so likewise does He give Himself wholly to us under the form of Wine for the "refreshing of our souls"—to cheer and to gladden us—even as David exclaims in the Psalm of the good Shepherd,[1] "*et Calix meus inebrians, quam præclarus est!*"

Thus, as Bishop Forbes truly says:—

"While the Sacrament under one kind conveys all graces necessary to salvation, the Chalice has a special grace of its own,—the grace of gladdening."

And further:—

"Both species together signify the plenitude of the heavenly feast and the perfect satisfaction of the soul, which each by itself does not signify."

[1] Ps. xxiii. 5.

"Granted that either species refects us by causing habitual grace, there are certain secondary effects of the spiritual meat and drink:—that of the meat is to strengthen the weak, as it is written, 'and bread to strengthen man's heart'; that of drink is to give joy to the sad, 'and wine that maketh glad the heart of man'[1] signifies that spiritual transport, that *inebriatio animæ*, of which Scripture speaks."[2]

As we are accustomed to sing:—

"And oh, what transport of delight
From Thy pure Chalice floweth!"[3]

We may conclude, therefore, that it is desirable to administer Communion under both kinds, wherever practicable, in order that the faithful may participate in the more abundant fruits of this holy Sacrament; while at the same time it is legitimate to administer the same under either kind in exceptional cases, so that all graces necessary to salvation may be conveyed to all who devoutly desire to receive this heavenly food.

2. This conclusion is supported by the following historical considerations. First, the usual mention of bread, when the Eucharist was reserved by the faithful in the earliest days of the Church, would lead us to infer that it was then received privately under that species only. There would even seem to be Scriptural warrant for this usage in the well-

---

[1] Ps. civ. 15.

[2] *Cf. Explanation of the Thirty-nine Articles*, Art. xxx., *Of both kinds*, p. 599.

[3] See version of Ps. xxiii. by the late Rev. Sir Henry Baker, Bart., *Hymns Ancient and Modern*, No. 197.

known reference to daily Communion in the Acts of the Apostles, wherein we read that the first Christians, in the Church at Jerusalem, continued "daily with one accord in the Temple, and breaking the Bread from house to house"; or, as it is rendered in the margin, "*at Home*."[1] Thus leading us to infer that the Eucharist was daily celebrated in the Home of the infant Church, that large upper Room, furnished and prepared, where the perpetual Sacrifice of the new law had been divinely instituted; and that the Bread thus hallowed was, at the conclusion of the Divine Liturgy, carried by the faithful "from house to house" for the Communion of the sick or of the absent, who were thus enabled to participate in the sacramental blessings of communion in the Body of Christ; in that they were "all partakers of that one Bread."[2]

We learn from S. Justin Martyr,[3] in the second

[1] Acts ii. 46. It may indeed be questioned whether the phrase—κατ' οἶκον—strictly means "from house to house," although there would seem to be sufficient precedent for this interpretation; and the reading in the Vulgate—*frangentes circa domos panem*—certainly supports the Authorised Version. Moreover, it is clear from the reference to the Sunday Eucharist at Troas—Acts xx. 7—and to 1 Cor. x. 16, that, in the minds of the translators, "the Bread" thus broken was indeed "the Communion of the Body of Christ."

[2] 1 Cor. x. 17.

[3] *Cf.* Apol. I. 65—67 (Oxford Translation, 1836). It is plain from Justin Martyr that the Eucharistic Elements were received in both kinds in the public ministration; but his words do not necessarily imply that they were thus sent to the absent, especially when we remember the apparent usage of the Apostolic Church; and also that, in the earliest times when Christians were permitted to carry home the

century, that it was certainly the practice of the Church in the sub-Apostolic age thus to send the Eucharist by the hands of the deacons to those who were debarred from presenting themselves for Communion in the solemn assemblies of the faithful. It would therefore seem that the primitive usage of Reservation, and of thus giving Communion to the absent under the species of Bread, is really co-eval with Christianity itself.

It is also true that, while the Eucharist was anciently reserved with great honour in the churches under both kinds, it was only exceptionally administered to the sick under the species of Wine; namely, in cases where, by reason of infirmity, the sick were unable to swallow the consecrated Bread. Thus the fourth Council of Carthage ordained that "the Eucharist be *poured* into the mouth" of any who may be afflicted with frenzy :— "*Infundatur ori ejus Eucharistia.*"[1] Children also, as we learn from S. Cyprian and S. Augustine, were communicated immediately after their baptism, with the Lord's most precious Blood.[2]

Lord's Body, veiled in "a fair linen cloth," known as the *Dominicum*, there is no recorded reference to the use of a phial, or similar vessel, for reserving the precious Blood. Tertullian, SS. Basil, Cyprian, and Augustine all bear witness to the same usage as the ordinary custom of the Church. *Cf.* Bp. Forbes on the Articles, pp. 569, 597.

[1] Canon 76; see *The Union Review*, vol. VIII. p. 422.

[2] S. Cyprian, *De Lapsis*, vi. 16; S. Augustine, *De Trinitate*, lib. iv. c. 10.

For this purpose, doubtless, the consecrated Element of Wine was reserved at Milan, as S. Augustine testifies¹ (*in Doliis aureis*), in golden barrel-shaped vessels; the like custom was also observed at Constantinople in the fourth century.

Probably few incidents in ecclesiastical history present a more terrible picture of the evils of Erastianism, particularly when joined in an unholy alliance with so-called religious and political fanaticism, than that referred to by S. Chrysostom in his letter to Pope Innocent; from which we learn that while he was administering Holy Baptism on Easter Eve (*in Sabbato Sancto*) in the great church of Santa Sophia,² the Arian and Manichæan mercenaries of Theophilus, the turbulent patriarch of Alexandria, broke into the House of God, under orders from the Emperor, and, penetrating into the sanctuary, rifled the Aumbrey wherein the Blessed Sacrament was reserved; whence they tore the Holy of Holies and poured forth the precious Blood of Christ upon their raiment,³ as though "counting the Blood of the Covenant an unholy thing."⁴

No profanation surely, which has shocked the instinctive reverence of Englishmen in the great

¹ *Epist.* IV. 4.

² The Patriarchal Church of S. Sophia, founded by Constantine the Great, but subsequently rebuilt by the Emperor Justinian.

³ "*Et sanctissimus Christi sanguis in prædictorum vestes effundebatur.*"—*Epist. S. Chrysostomi ad Innocent. PP.*, I. p. 783.

⁴ Heb. x. 29.

upheaval of the sixteenth century, or in more recent times, could exceed this terrible act of sacrilege, perpetrated by lapsed Christians,—not only with the connivance of Arian, but even of Catholic bishops, actuated by a temporising policy; at the instigation of a Christian Emperor and the Empress Eudoxia who, stirred by revenge, shrank not from so great a wickedness, even while claiming the privilege, though grievously forgetful of the duty, appertaining to "nursing fathers" and "nursing mothers" in the Church of God.[1]

Notwithstanding "our unhappy divisions" and the serious evils resulting from the lax observance of ecclesiastical discipline, and from long-standing confusion as to the canonical and legislative functions of the Spiritualty and Temporalty respectively, it must thankfully be admitted that no such tremendous scandal has disgraced the annals of our time. But the inference is obvious, viz. that difficulties, with which we all are familiar, were experienced when the Empire had become Christian, and the visible unity of the Church was still unbroken. Chrysostom, be it remembered, was uncanonically deposed and died in exile, his end being accelerated by the hardships to which he was cruelly subjected. Thus Erastianism, investing (as it does) the Temporal power with an unconstitutional supremacy in Spiritual things, affected the Church in the fourth and fifth

[1] Isai. xlix. 23.

centuries no less than in the nineteenth; and must be regarded as the expression of that fundamental hostility with which, in one form or another, the world-power is ever seeking to circumvent and to destroy the heaven-born energy of the Supernatural Kingdom of God Incarnate.

But to return. Early in the fifth century we find a touching account of the last Communion of S. Mary of Egypt, recorded in the *Lives of the Saints*.[1] We are told that towards the close of her life-long penance in the wilderness beyond Jordan, the Abbot Zosimus took to her on Maundy Thursday, about the year A.D. 430, in a small chalice and under both kinds, the saving Mysteries of the Lord's Body and Blood. And that after receiving her Lord God Incarnate in His holy Sacrament,—

> "There present, in the heart
> As in the hands,"[2]—

this saint and penitent in holy transport, like Simeon of old with the world's Redeemer in his arms, said aloud her *Nunc dimittis* in thanksgiving for her Communion.

The same custom likewise prevailed in Britain in the fourth and fifth centuries. From the *Reliquiæ Celticæ Liturgicæ* we learn that the sick were

---

[1] *Cf.* Alban Butler's *Lives of the Saints*, S. Mary of Egypt, April 9th.

[2] *The Christian Year*, authorised edition, published by Messrs. Parker (London, 1866).

usually communicated under both kinds, and may infer from the liturgical fragments preserved in the Scottish Book of Deer and the Irish Books of Dimma and Mulling, entitled respectively "*Missa de Infirmis*," whereas in the Stowe Missal the corresponding office is entitled "*Ordo ad Cammunicandum Infirmum*," that this usage was observed whether Communion was given with the reserved Sacrament or when Mass was celebrated in the sick man's presence. It is also evident, from the rubrics and *formulæ* of administration, that the Eastern custom of giving the Eucharist under both species simultaneously was then observed in Britain. Thus in the Book of Mulling, and similarly in the Book of Deer:—

"*Tum reficitur Corpore et Sanguine.*

"*Corpus cum Sanguine Domini nostri Jesu Christi sanitas sit tibi in vitam æternam.*"

In the Book of Dimma, and also in the Stowe Missal, the *formula* of administration is:—

"*Corpus et Sanguis D.N.J.C. filii Dei vivi conservat animam tuam in vitam æternam.*"[1]

It would thus appear, from the historical and liturgical notices of this subject subsequent to the days of persecution, when the customs of the Church became more settled, that the Eucharist was ordinarily reserved under both species, and that in

[1] *Cf. The Liturgy and Ritual of the Celtic Church*, by Rev. F. E. Warren, B.D., pp. 138, 139, 164, 167, 170, 173, 223, 224.

certain places, as in the East and in the Isles of Britain, it was thus administered to the sick and absent.

We have evidence of the continuance of the same custom in the Church of England in Anglo-Saxon times. For example, it is recorded by S. Bede that a certain officer or prefect at the Court of Egbert, king of Northumbria, named Hildmaer, specially dear to the blessed Cuthbert (*a Beato Cuthberto specialiter dilectus*), besought the Bishop to send a priest to visit his wife, who seemed to be at the point of death, and to minister to her the Sacraments of the Lord's Body and Blood:—

"Obsecro, quia uxor mea male habet et videtur jam proxima morti, ut mittas presbyterum qui illam priusquam moriatur visitet, *eique Corporis et Sanguinis Dominici sacramenta ministret;* sed et corpus ipsius hic locis sanctis sepiliri permittas."[1]

Moreover, we have already learned, from the same venerable historian and doctor of the English Church, that S. Cuthbert himself received the Viaticum under both species (*vide*, p. 17, note). Hence it follows that the Communion of the sick under both kinds was no mere peculiarity of the British Church, since both SS. Cuthbert and Bede had themselves conformed to the Roman usages introduced by S. Augustine, which were adopted in Northumbria at the Synod of Whitby, A.D. 664.

[1] *Cf.* BEDÆ HIST. ECCLES., *Vita Sancti Patris, Monachi simul et Antistitis, Cuthberti,* cap. xv (Cambridge, 1722).

In fact, the custom of reserving the Blessed Sacrament under both species, whether separately or conjointly, was retained into the Middle Ages, until the misapplication of the doctrine of concomitance restricted the communion of the chalice to the celebrating priest. Thus we are told that in the eleventh century the monks of Cluny, like the Abbot Zosimus when taking Communion under both kinds to S. Mary of Egypt, were in the habit of using a *chalice*, covered with a white veil (*mundo velamine*), in carrying the Viaticum to the sick and dying[1]; and that early in the twelfth century Pope Paschal II., in writing to one of that Order, directed that any sick persons who, by reason of their infirmity, could not consume the sacred Host, should be communicated under the species of Wine.[2] Hence the use of a chalice, mentioned in the historical notices of conveying the reserved Sacrament to the sick, as in the above reference to the practice of the Cluniac Brethren, especially when coupled with the subsequent direction given by Pope Paschal II., may be regarded as evidence that the Eucharist was then

---

[1] *Cf.* D'Achery, *Spicilegium*, tom. IV.; *Contumes de Cluny*, lib. III. c. xxviii.

[2] *Epist.* III., ad *Pontium Cluniacensem*. See two interesting articles in the *Union Review* for September, 1870, and March, 1871, *On Ciboriums and the Reservation of the Blessed Sacrament;* also a valuable essay, entitled *Reservation of the Blessed Sacrament*, by the late Rev. Canon Humble, Precentor of Perth Cathedral, to be found in *Studies in Modern Problems* (London, 1874); to which the reader is referred for further information.

administered to the sick under both kinds, and as pointing to the conclusion that down to the eleventh and twelfth centuries the Eucharist was not unfrequently reserved under both species; or at least, even supposing that the Viaticum was more generally given under the form of Bread, that in cases of necessity the sick and dying were communicated with our Lord's most precious Blood.

3. In passing to the further consideration of this question in its practical bearings, it is important to observe that the Catholic usage of administering Holy Communion under both kinds was restored in England by the concurrent action of the Spiritualty and Temporalty in the Convocation and Parliament of 1547.

This restoration of the ancient custom, having been approved unanimously in Convocation, was enacted by Parliament in the following terms :—

"And forasmuch as it is more agreeable, both to the first institution of the said Sacrament of the most precious Body and Blood of our Saviour Jesus Christ, and also more conformable to the common use and practice both of the Apostles, and of the Primitive Church by the space of five hundred years and more after Christ's ascension, that the Blessed Sacrament should be ministered to all Christian people under both the kinds of bread and wine, than under the form of bread only; and also it is more agreeable to the first institution of Christ, and to the usage of the Apostles and the Primitive Church, that the people being present should receive the same with the Priest, than that the Priest should receive it alone; therefore be it enacted by our Sovereign Lord the King, with the consent of the Lords Spiritual and Temporal, and the Commons in this present Parliament assembled, and by the authority of the same, that the said most blessed Sacrament be hereafter commonly delivered and ministered unto the people within the Church of England and Ireland, and other the King's Dominions, under both the kinds, that is to say, of bread and wine, *except necessity otherwise require*, . . . not condemning hereby the usage of any Church out of the King's Majesties Dominions."[1]

Here it is worthy of note, as Dr. Lingard points out, that this legislative sanction of the practice of Communion under both kinds "permits Communion under one kind when necessity may require it, and professes not to censure any foreign Church which may retain the contrary practice."[2]

This Act of 1547 was repealed upon the accession of Mary, but having been revived in 1558, upon the accession of Elizabeth, remains in force at the present time.[3] Hence it has co-ordinate authority with the Acts of Uniformity of 1559 and 1661; and therefore Communion under either kind, in cases of necessity continues to be authorised under the established Order of this Church and Realm; moreover, the use of the ancient terminology, such as "*the Sacrament of the Altar*" and the term "*Altar*" when applied to the Lord's Table, is thus seen to possess legislative sanction; a consideration

---

[1] *Cf.* 1 Edw. VI. Cap. 1, *An Act against such as shall unreverently speak against the Sacrament of the Altar, and of receiving thereof under both kinds.*

[2] *Cf.* Dr. Lingard's *History of England*, vol. VII. p. 23.

[3] *Cf.* Bishop Gibson's *Codex Juris Eccles. Anglicani*, I. xx. pp. 462, 480.

which ought surely to have weight in certain quarters, where it has been too readily assumed that the process of appealing to Temporal authority, respecting Spiritual things, must necessarily result in demonstrating the illegality of Catholic observance in the Church of England; an assumption which more accurate acquaintance with the Ecclesiastical Law, particularly when illustrated by impartial historical research, would have proved to be entirely without foundation.

This joint action on the part of the Spiritualty and Temporalty, which resulted in the Order of Communion published by authority in 1548, had reference exclusively to the public administration of the holy Sacrament. It did not therefore in any way touch the Reservation of the Blessed Sacrament as enjoined in the Provincial Constitution of Archbishop Peccham. Moreover, when we remember that the Order of Communion was incorporated in the accustomed Ordinary and Canon of the Mass, according to the Sarum Rite, and that no office for private celebration for the sick was in use before Whitsuntide 1549, it is obvious that the former custom of communicating the sick with the reserved Sacrament (*sub latibulo panis*), under the form of Bread, as provided by the Ecclesiastical Law, would still continue to be observed; a conclusion which is strengthened by the *proviso* in the Act of 1547, giving legislative sanction to the administration of

Holy Communion under both kinds, "*except necessity otherwise require*"; an exception which must be taken to include the Communion of the sick and dying.

In the Order for the Communion of the Sick in the Prayer Book of 1549, it is provided that "*the Priest shall reserve so much of the Sacrament of the Body and Blood as shall serve the sick person, and so many as shall communicate with him, if there be any.*" These words do not explicitly order Communion under both kinds, although they undoubtedly sanction such administration, the phrase "*Sacrament of the Body and Blood*" being a technical expression, used with reference to either kind, inasmuch as it is clearly stated in this Book, as we have before observed, that "*in each of them*" is received "*the whole Body of our Saviour Jesus Christ.*" The same form of expression is also used by Bishop Tunstall in his Visitation of the Church of Durham (*vide supra*, pp. 59, 62), when ordaining that, "according to the sacred canons, *the Sacrament of the Body and Blood of our Lord Jesus Christ* be in future reserved in a decent Tabernacle, over against the High Altar." We also find corroborative evidence in support of this interpretation in the Latin version of the above rubric given in the Book of 1560:—"*tunc Sacerdos . . . . tantum Sacramenti servabit, quantum sufficit ægroto.*" Whence it appears that no explicit direction has been given enjoining the administration of the Eucharist under both kinds, when the sick are communicated with the reserved Sacrament, and that in such cases of necessity Communion may be given under the form of Bread, as provided in the Provincial Constitution and sanctioned in the Act of 1547.

Of course, whenever the Eucharist is celebrated in presence of the sick, the Communion is to be administered under both kinds, as enjoined in the public Order of the Church; unless indeed the sick be unable to swallow solid food, in which case he would be communicated with the Sacrament of the Lord's Body and Blood, under the species of Wine, as formerly enjoined by Pope Paschal II. But in order to provide for the exigencies of the sick and dying, it would, upon the whole, appear to be desirable, on the ground of reverence and practical convenience, that the Eucharist should commonly be reserved in the pyx within the Tabernacle under the form of Bread, and so be reverently carried to the sick in cases of emergency, as provided in the Ecclesiastical Law. Whereas, in cases where "*timely notice*" can be given,—that is "*over night or else early in the morning*" —it is advisable that the Eucharist be reserved under both kinds at the public Celebration, and so be ministered to the sick; and that if by reason of distance, or upon

---

[1] *Cf. Communion of the Sick* in Prayer Books of 1549, 1552, and 1559.

other sufficient grounds, the two kinds cannot be reverently conveyed separately, they may be administered conjointly by *intinction*. This, indeed, is the custom observed in the Eastern Church at the present time.

Thus we come to the conclusion, suggested by the above theological, historical, and practical considerations, that whereas Communion under both kinds is undoubtedly more conformable to the Divine Institution of the Eucharistic Mystery, and more agreeable to the general tradition of the Church, as the normal usage to be observed in her public Liturgy, and as far as practicable in all private ministrations, nevertheless that, concurrently with this uniform tradition, there is abundant precedent for Communion under either kind in the exceptional cases of the sick and dying, since under either species all saving grace is conveyed to the soul, and that such cases of necessity are recognised by the Ecclesiastical Law of England.

CHAPTER VI.

SUMMARY AND CONCLUSION.

IN concluding the argument in support of the Anglican authority for the Reservation of the Blessed Sacrament, the following considerations appear to invite attention; in which we will endeavour to sum up the statements and arguments which have already been advanced in the preceding chapters of this Treatise.

1.

In the first place the author desires to state that, while respectfully deprecating any action on the part of their lordships the bishops, which would have the appearance of deviating from that fidelity to Catholic principle and primitive usage which distinguished their predecessors of the Restoration period; on the other hand he feels bound to add, that he does not advocate any ill-advised or precipitate revival of this custom on the part of the parochial clergy. That this "laudable practice of the Church of England" in former days, and "indeed of the whole Catholic Church of Christ," will be eventually restored amongst us there can be no

Ill-advised action deprecated, either in forbidding or restoring Reservation.

reasonable doubt. To those who can read the signs of the times, and recognise the interior working of God's Holy Spirit in our midst during the last fifty years of ecclesiastical life in England; and discern the gracious purposes for which the historic Church in this land is destined in these latter days as "The repairer of the breach, The restorer of paths to dwell in;"[1] and as designed to be in truth the peacemaker to the universal Church and to the whole world; it is evident that this Catholic and primitive usage will in God's good time be restored among us, just as the ecclesiastical spirit among our clergy, and the discipline of the spiritual life among our people, and the august solemnities of divine worship have been, and are now being, continually and with everincreasing perfection and beauty restored in our Communion. We may therefore well afford to be patient, and ought reverently to take heed, lest by inconsiderate action, either in attempting to hinder or to anticipate what is manifestly in other hands and under Divine guidance, we be found haply to be counselling or to be working against God.

2.

Importance of the observance of the sixth Post-communion rubric.

In the next place he would venture respectfully to submit that the strict and conscientious observance of the sixth Post-communion rubric will best prepare us for the inestimable privilege and blessing

[1] Isai. lviii. 12.

of the reserved Sacrament in our churches. Obedience is the surest path to true progress and to ecclesiastical reform. It is not, in short, by systematically or inconsiderately breaking the law, but by the exact observance of the law that we shall best promote that temper of deference to authority and distrust of self, which is an absolute and indispensable condition in securing an equitable readjustment and lasting improvement in ecclesiastical affairs.

(i) This rubric, like that which precedes the Post-communion, is a witness to the permanent sacredness of the consecrated Elements, and therefore directs that "if any remain of that which was consecrated," it shall be "reverently" received and consumed, as Lyndwood says, "by the priest and his ministers" (saving what might be required for the Communion of the Sick); or as Bishop Cosin adds, "by the communicants in the church" (*vid. sup.* pp. 29, 30, 35, 36).

It is not the author's wish to institute comparisons; but is it not too notorious that they who disapprove of Reservation, upon the ground that it is forbidden by this rubric, are for the most part the very persons who are themselves indifferent to the careful observance, in this respect, of the prescribed Order of the Church? Are there not too many who, while straining the cautionary provision here enjoined, lest any of the consecrated Elements "might," as Bishop Cosin says, "be put to any common use," and for that purpose " be carried out of the church," into a virtual prohibition of reserving any that may be needed for the Communion of the sick and dying, give but little heed to the explicit direction that whatever is not so required is to be "*reverently*" consumed? Are not churchmen pained, it may be on great occasions or at important ecclesiastical functions, by an example of indifference such as would be regarded in social life as want of good breeding, or at least of good manners, on the part of some of the higher clergy in leaving the Altar of God—the Table of the Great King—without scrupulous and devout care in observing His own admonition, to "gather up the fragments that remain, that nothing be lost"?[1]

(ii) It must also be observed that this rubric is very precise in its terms in directing that "the priest," *i.e.* the celebrant, "and" if need be, "such other communicants as he shall then call unto him, shall immediately after the Blessing reverently eat and drink" any of the consecrated species that may remain. And further, as we have previously noted, that it simply carries on the practice which had been traditional in the Western Church from days of remote antiquity [*vid. sup.* Chap. IV. 2 (iii) p. 83] in thus providing for the reverent consumption of the consecrated Elements which may not be required

[1] St. John vi. 12.

for the Communion of the Sick. This rule, together with that which is still enjoined in the Canon Law of the Church of England, in the Constitution of Archbishop Edmund (*vid. sup.* p. 27, note), directing that the priest—*post celebrationem Missæ tam Patinam quam Calicem faciat aqua perfundi*, for which purpose he is to have at hand *pannum mundidissimum*, . . . *in quo post susceptionem Sacramenti salutaris digitos cum labiis ablutos emundet*,[1]—supplies a complete guide to the reverent and becoming fulfilment of this duty according to the established Order of the Church in this land.

Some there may be who hitherto have refrained from taking the prescribed Ablutions, not from any lack of reverence for the holy Sacrament, but because this observance is not explicitly enjoined in the rubric. It may not therefore be amiss to point out, with Bishop Cosin,[2] that the appointed Order of the Church is contained not only in the *Book of Common Prayer*, but also in the Provincial Constitutions and Canons Ecclesiastical; and that this particular custom of cleansing the sacred vessels, which indeed is necessarily implied in the present rubric, continued to be observed, together with other

[1] *Cf.* Lyndwood, *Provinciale*, pp. 234, 235; also Bp. Gibson's *Codex*, vol. I. 480. From which it would appear that this Constitution, which is still *legally* in force, had become obsolete in practice during the last century.

[2] *Cf.* Cosin's Works, *Notes on the Book of Common Prayer*, Third Series, p. 439.

Catholic usages under the Prayer Book of 1549. Thus Cosin, to whose accurate knowledge and diligence we are so greatly indebted for information respecting the successive alterations in the *Book of Common Prayer*, tells us that Bucer "likewise finds fault with those ministers that still used vestments and lights in the church; with the gestures of bowing and crossing; *with making clean the chalice;* taking the bread and wine into the priest's hand when he repeats the words of institution over them; removing the Service Book from the right to the left side of the table; setting the table in the same place where the altar stood; and with shewing the bread and cup to old doting and superstitious persons who were ready to adore them."

"All which he wished to have altered; and so it was in the 5th of Edward VI. But in the beginning of Queen Elizabeth all the ornaments of the Church were restored again by the Act of Uniformity, and the posture of the table where the Altar stood was specially appointed by the queen's injunctions."[1]

---

[1] *Ibid.* p. 418. Bucer's words are:—"Sunt quibuscunque possunt signis, nunquam satis execratam Missam suam repræsentare student et vestibus, luminaribus, et inclinationibus, crucibus, *abluendo calicem*, aliisque Missalibus gestibus, halitu super panem et calicem Eucharistiæ, transferendo librum in mensa de dextra ad sinistram mensæ partem, mensam in eodem ponendo loco quo stabat altare: ostendendo panem et calicem Eucharistiæ, adorantibus illa vetulis aliisque superstitiosis hominibus qui Sacramentis tamen non communicant."—Bucer, *Censura in Ordinatione Eccl. in Anglia*, p. 494.

It is therefore evident that this ancient usage of thus cleansing the chalice and paten, like the custom of Reservation, rested originally upon the traditional practice or unwritten law of the Church, and was subsequently regulated and enjoined by the Canon Law before it was prescribed in the rubrics. In this respect our present Order is in substantial agreement with the usages of Catholic antiquity. In this light therefore must this sixth Post-communion rubric be regarded; not as forbidding any "laudable practice" then permitted, but as providing for the continuance of the traditional custom of the Church in reverently consuming whatever might remain of the consecrated Elements.

(iii) The carelessness however, not to say irreverence, with which this Order of the Church is neglected or disobeyed by many who most strongly object to the Reservation of the holy Mysteries, shews that there is a serious unreality and inconsistency in simply making use of this rubric as an argument against Reservation. With such persons this objection, it must be feared, does not arise from any conscientious obedience to authority, or from any newly-aroused spirit of enthusiasm in promoting the exact observance of rubrics which had unhappily been long regarded as a dead letter. It is alas but too evident, that both disobedience to the Order enjoined in this rubric and opposition to the primitive custom of reserving the Blessed Sacrament for the sick spring from the same root, viz. from lack of faith in failing to realise the inherent sacredness of the consecrated Elements, in consequence of the real and objective presence, beneath these sacramental veils, of the precious Body and Blood of God Incarnate. This is in truth, for the most part, the fundamental error wherein the various arguments against the practice of Reservation take their root, however speciously they may be veiled under the pretext of obedience to the appointed Order of the Church, as set forth in this rubric, and in the prescribed Order for the Communion of the Sick, or in the assumed prohibition of Reservation in the twenty-eighth Article of Religion. And this fundamental truth of the real presence of God Incarnate, Whose " delight is to be with the sons of men "[1] in all the fulness of His divine and human personality, communicating Himself to us "to be our spiritual food and sustenance in that holy Sacrament,"[2] supporting the sick and bringing comfort and protection to the dying;—this is also the ground whereon the advocates of Reservation take their stand.

(iv) Further, the documentary evidence of Bishop Cosin's Visitation Articles and Notes on the Common Prayer demonstrates that this sixth Post-communion rubric was intended as a safeguard against the

[1] *Cf.* Prov. viii. 31. *Et deliciæ Meæ esse cum filiis hominum.*
[2] Exhortation in Communion Office.

profanation of the Blessed Sacrament (*vide supra*, pp. 9—12); while therefore we are barred by its history from regarding it as forbidding Reservation, there can be no doubt whatever as to the obligation which it lays upon the clergy of carefully and reverently consuming whatever may remain of the consecrated Elements, over and above any that may be required for purposes of Communion. It is therefore submitted that they who disregard the plain and significant directions of this rubric are not in a position to forbid the practice of Reservation. Obviously, the point of primary importance enjoined by this rubric is the provision that "if any remain of that which was consecrated," it shall be "reverently" and devoutly consumed; the direction that "it shall not be carried out of the Church" is strictly antithetical to "the Curate shall have it to his own use," in the preceding clause, respecting any that may "remain unconsecrated." Thus the "unconsecrated" may "be carried out of the Church," because, being "unconsecrated," "the curate shall have it to his own use"; whereas the *consecrated* "may not be put to any common use" (*vid. sup.* p. 29), and *for this end* "it shall not be carried out of the Church," *i.e.* in order that the curate may "have it home to his house,"—a scandal still existing among the Puritan clergy in 1661; concerning which Cosin (who then adopted this prohibition from the Scotch Liturgy) had previously enquired in his Visitation Articles of 1627. We have also seen that about 1640 Cosin again refers to the same scandal in his suggested correction of the rubric as it then stood:—*And if any of the bread and wine remain, the curate shall have it to his own use.* "Which words," Cosin adds, "some curates have abused and extended so far that they suppose they may take all that remains of the consecrated Bread and Wine itself home to their houses, and there eat and drink the same with their other common meats. .... And therefore," as he proceeds, "some words are needful here to be added, whereby the priest may be enjoined to consider the number of them which are to receive the Sacrament, and to consecrate the bread and wine in such a near proportion as shall be sufficient for them; but if any of the consecrated Elements be left, that he and some others with him shall decently eat and drink them in the Church before all the people depart from it."[1]

These *Considerations*, as we learn from Dr. Nicholls at the end of his *Additional Notes on the Common Prayer*, published in 1709, were for the most part adopted by the Revisers in 1661. Hence it is plain that there was then no question of forbidding the primitive custom of reserving the Sacrament for the sick, in adopting the injunction that "it shall not be carried out of the Church." The

---

[1] *Cf.* Cosin's Works, vol. v., *Particulars to be Considered, Explained, and Corrected in the Book of Common Prayer*, p. 519.

Summary and Conclusion.

irregularities with which the bishops then had to deal were caused by the scandalous irreverence of the Puritans, not by any illegal or ill-considered restoration of Catholic observances. From this *Consideration* (which is in substantial agreement with Lyndwood's gloss upon the latter part of Archbishop Peccham's Constitution of 1281) it is also plain that, inasmuch as "the priest is enjoined to consider the number of them which are to receive the Sacrament," and by the present Offertory rubric is directed to place upon the Lord's Table "so much bread and wine as he shall think sufficient"; and further, since it is provided in the Provincial Constitution (referred to by Cosin as "being still in force") that, every Sunday at the least, the priest shall reserve so much of the consecrated Elements as may suffice for the probable needs of the sick in the week following; this corresponding provision in the present rubric—"if any remain of that which was consecrated"—must of necessity be limited to "any of the consecrated Elements which be left," beyond that which the priest shall think sufficient for the Communion of the sick and dying. "If any" thus "remain of that which was consecrated, it shall not be carried out of the Church, but," as this rubric (following the former Constitution) enjoins, "the priest and (if need be) some others with him," either his ministers (as directed in Lyndwood's gloss) or "such other of the communicants as he shall then call unto him, shall immediately after the Blessing reverently eat and drink the same."

(v) In thus summing up the consideration of this rubric, in the light of history and with due regard for the requirements of our Ecclesiastical Law, the writer is aware that nothing he can say will prove conclusive to those who do not wish to be convinced of the lawfulness of Reservation, according to the established Order of this Church and Realm. Such persons will continue to shelter themselves under the modern and superficial interpretation of the mere *words* of this sixth rubric, divorced from its history and from the primitive and canonical discipline in which it originated. At the same time he confidently hopes that he may commend to unprejudiced minds the historical, liturgical, and legal considerations suggested in this Treatise, as tending, at any rate, to establish the conclusion that the Reservation of the Blessed Sacrament for the Sick is authorised in the Church of England; and that this particular rubric, which is commonly supposed to forbid the practice of Reservation, is in substantial agreement with the Provincial Constitution which enjoins and regulates this primitive and Catholic observance.

3.

The principle of Reservation recognised in the English rite. In order to arrive at a right conclusion, it is also to be remembered that the offices, rubrics, and other formularies of the Church must be regarded as exhibiting a uniform system of faith, devotion, and observance. They are therefore to be interpreted by one uniform method of scriptural, historical, and liturgical elucidation. Hence historical considerations may not be set aside in one case, nor liturgical examination in another; nor is it reasonable to ignore both history and primitive usage in order to build up a modern theory upon the narrow basis of the *litera scripta* of any given rubric. Therefore this sixth rubric must be taken in conjunction with that which, having been adopted at the same time, immediately precedes the Post-communion, directing that—"*When all have communicated, the minister shall return to the Lord's Table and reverently place upon it what remaineth of the consecrated Elements, covering the same with a fair linen cloth.*"

(i) In this rubric, as we have already demonstrated [*vid. sup.* Chap. III. 3 (ii)], the principle of Reservation is explicitly recognised in the very remarkable counterpart to the liturgical customs of antiquity, which is here presented by the English rite; while in the Ornaments rubric and preface concerning Ceremonies the same principle is intrinsically recognised, because both refer to a time when the practice of Reservation was distinctly enjoined in the Order for the Communion of the Sick, and undoubtedly practised (*Cf.* pp. 21—25). Now this primitive custom of reserving part of the Eucharist until the end of Mass, to which the same custom enjoined in our present English rite is analogous, is distinctly referred to by ancient writers as the *reserved* Sacrament. Thus :—*Secundum Gelasium Papam,* . . . *pars reservata usque in finem missæ, secundum antiquum ecclesiæ Romanæ morem, pro ministris vel infirmis, significat omnes mortuos.*

Again, in the Treatise by Micrologus :—

"Tertium quod jam requiescit in Christo, quod etiam in tertia particula *in altari reservata* apte figuratur, *quam viaticum morientium apellare solemus.*"

Moreover, the object of this reservation is here plainly set forth;—*pro ministris vel infirmis* by Gelasius, while the Eucharist thus reserved upon the altar is referred to as *viaticum morientium* by Micrologus.

This same liturgical observance was enjoined in the English rite in 1661, and although, as we have already seen (*cf.* pp. 36—46), the immediate object of this rubric was to provide for the Reservation of the Eucharist until after the Blessing, in order that the propitiatory sacrifice of Christ's death and passion might be pleaded, His Godhead worshipped, and His Blessing bestowed, in union with the Oblation of His holy Mysteries,—it is inconceivable that those learned prelates and divines, who thus enjoined the primitive usage of reserving the Eucharist until the end of Mass, could have intended in a subsequent rubric, drawn up at the same time to provide for the reverent consumption of the consecrated Elements, to prohibit that Reservation for the sick and dying for which this liturgical usage was originally designed.

(ii) The absence from this sixth rubric of distinct provision for the continued Reservation for the sick is easily accounted for by the fact, that in 1661 the complete system of ecclesiastical discipline and Catholic observance could only be slowly and painfully restored, after the entire proscription throughout the length and breadth of the land of Divine Service, and the terrible profanation of sacred things caused by the great Rebellion, which for a time overthrew the monarchy, together with the external organisation of the Church. The cathedrals and parish churches were in several places in ruins, while in many instances the benefices were still held by Puritan ministers. Under such conditions it was impossible to do more than maintain the fundamental principles of faith and discipline involved in the Divine Constitution of the Church of Christ, and to insist upon the *minimum* of decency in the Service of the Church; leaving both the development of those principles and the restoration of the ancient ceremonial in the hands of God, to be restored in the course of His providence and according to the purposes of His will. Thus, in a calm spirit of unwavering faith, the great prelates of the Restoration period with wonderful wisdom and foresight, under the guidance of the Holy Ghost, laid the foundation of that ecclesiastical revival in the midst of which we are privileged to live. As in the Ornaments rubric they prepared for the eventual restoration of the ancient ceremonial, so frequently referred to (in Cosin's *Notes on the Common Prayer*) as still enjoined by the Order of this Church and Realm (although at the same time they did not force matters, nor fully restore the solemnities of Divine Service, for which they advisedly made provision), so likewise with regard to Reservation, while they enshrined in the Eucharistic Office the principle of thus reserving the holy Mysteries, and herein restored the primitive usage of reserving the Eucharist until the end of the Divine Service, for the Communion of the sick and dying; they gave no explicit direction for the application of this principle, and contented themselves with providing in the subsequent rubric for the reverent consumption of the consecrated Elements, without special reference to any that might be reserved for the Communion of the sick, but without prohibiting such Reservation. The result of this singular fidelity, moderation, and wisdom on the part of the Caroline divines is the significant fact, which we are only just beginning to realise, that the primitive usage of Reservation is enshrined in our English Liturgy; whence it necessarily follows that a principle thus publicly recognised, according to the Order of the Church at every Celebration, cannot be regarded as contrary to her spirit, intention, and discipline, when practically carried out to its legitimate conclusion. And thus, in the significant words of a philosophical writer, quoted nearly half a century ago by Cardinal Newman:—"More was done than even yet appears in the Convocation of 1661."

4.

The like considerations also explain the absence of explicit reference to Reservation in the appointed Order for the Communion of the Sick.

Concerning the Order for the Communion of the Sick, and the evidence of Bp. Sparrow.

(i) Here it must be remembered that no directions for the Communion of the sick with the reserved Sacrament were *omitted* in the Revision of 1661. All that was then done was to amend the rubrics of the then existing Order in the *English Book of Common Prayer*, which provided for Celebration in the sick man's house; leaving the ancient custom of Reservation exactly where it was before, viz. as resting upon primitive tradition, as being still enjoined by the Ecclesiastical Law, and as distinctly recognised in the Latin Prayer Book, "which," as Wheatley observes, "was put out by authority in the second year of Queen Elizabeth."[1]

(ii) In addition to the considerations already suggested as bearing upon this question [*vide supra*, Chap. IV. 2 (iii)], it is plain from Bishop Cosin's *Considerations*, which led the way to so many of the

---

[1] *Cf.* Wheatley on the *Common Prayer*, p. 482.

rubrical improvements adopted in 1661, that the emendations then made had reference *exclusively* to the then existing Order. The time was not opportune for replacing in the English Book of 1661 the rubrics directing Reservation for the sick from the Prayer Book of 1549, even if, upon other grounds, such an arrangement were thought desirable. Nor could the question of Reservation for the sick, dependent as it was upon frequent or at least weekly Celebration, come within the range of practical politics at a time when the appointed celebration "*in Cathedral and Collegiate Churches and Colleges, ... every Sunday at the least,*" was almost entirely unknown; and when the Oblation of the Eucharist, abroad in the country, was lamentably infrequent. Under such circumstances, the private Celebration for the sick was the only provision which could reasonably be entertained, and this indeed was imperative, if the sick were to be communicated at all.

(iii) It has indeed been urged, with some show of reason, that the rubrical corrections made in 1661 exclude the traditional custom of communicating the sick with the reserved Sacrament, which it is allowed was admissible before. But this theory is at once seen to be untenable when we refer to the corrections suggested by Bishop Cosin. His words are:—

"The Collect, Epistle, and Gospel is here specially

ordered, but what part of the public Order at the Communion is to be used, and what omitted (as some part of it seems needful to be), is not here said."[1]

To remedy this defect the following corrections were made in 1661, which, so far from excluding Reservation, were simply based upon the rubrics of 1549, providing for the reverent Celebration for the sick, in case there were no "open Communion in the Church" at which "the priest might reserve so much of the Sacrament of the Body and Blood" as would serve for the Communion of the sick.

In the Prayer Book of 1552, and again in that of 1559, the first rubric ended thus:—

"And having a convenient place in the sick man's house, where the Curate may reverently minister, *and a good number to receive the Communion with the sick person*, with all things necessary for the same, he shall there *minister* the holy Communion."

The corresponding rubric of 1549 had thus ended:—"he shall there *celebrate* the holy Communion *after such form and sort as hereafter is appointed.*"

Accordingly, in 1661, this rubric was re-cast in the following form:—

"And having a convenient place in the sick man's

[1] *Cf.* Cosin's Works, vol. v., *Corrections in the Prayer Book Suggested*, p. 524.

house, with all things necessary *so prepared*, that the Curate may reverently minister, he shall there *celebrate* the holy Communion, *beginning with the Collect, Epistle, and Gospel here following.*

Again, in the Book of 1559, immediately after the Gospel came the following rubric:—

"At the time of the distribution of the holy Sacrament the Priest shall first receive the Communion himself, and after minister unto them that be appointed to communicate with the sick."

Whereas in 1549, after the Gospel followed:—

The Preface.

The Lord be with you.

Lift up your hearts, etc.

Unto the end of the Canon.

Then followed the rubric (above cited) concerning "the distribution of the holy Sacrament," in which the delivery of the Communion to the sick was not merely implied, but distinctly ordered:— "*and then to the sick person.*"

So likewise, in our present Order, after the Gospel follows the rubric:—

"After which the Priest shall proceed according to the form before prescribed for the holy Communion, beginning at these words [*Ye that do truly, etc.*]."

These words, it is to be observed, now precede *The Preface*, whereas in 1549 they followed in the open Communion, together with the "*general Con-*

Summary and Conclusion. 151

fession and Absolution, with the comfortable sentences of Scripture," then specially appointed at the Communion with the reserved Sacrament. Thus in this respect this rubric of 1661 is substantially identical with the Order prescribed in 1549.

In the succeeding rubric, directing that "the Priest" who thus celebrates "shall first receive the Communion himself, and after minister unto them that are appointed to communicate with the sick," is added, "and last of all to the sick person"; which, as we have just seen, is likewise taken from the Book of 1549.

Consequently the above rubrical directions, adopted in 1661, were simply intended to indicate "what part of the public Order at the Communion is to be used, and what omitted"; without any reference whatever to the concurrent tradition of communicating the sick with the reserved Sacrament, as provided in the rubrics of 1549; which, "at Calvin's and Bucer's instance, were omitted in the review of the book 5 Edw. VI. as not accounted absolutely necessary." To which Cosin adds significantly, "I say omitted only, and not condemned"[1] (*vide supra*, pp. 13—17).

(iv) This conclusion is corroborated by the evidence of Bishop Sparrow, who was associated with Cosin in the Revision of 1661. Only four years before that memorable event he had issued his

[1] *Cf.* Works, vol. v. p. 12.

Rationale upon the Book of Common Prayer; in which his comment upon the rubric at the Communion of the Sick reminds us of Cosin's *Considerations*, which we have just been considering. Sparrow was a younger man than Cosin, but both had been contemporaries at Cambridge, where Cosin was sometime Master of Peterhouse, and Sparrow was Scholar, and then Fellow, of Queens'. Prynne tells us "that divers Schollars of other houses usually resorted to Peterhouse, some out of curiosity only to behold, others to learne and practise the Popish ceremonies and orders used in that Chappell."[1]

Sparrow certainly handed on that Catholic tradition which Cosin taught and practised so assiduously, and which he had himself received, as he tells us repeatedly, from "my lord and master, Dr. Overall."[2] It is therefore not improbable that

[1] *Canterbury's Doom*, pp. 73, 74. Quoted in Introduction to *Bishop Cosin's Correspondence*, vol. I. xxx., by the late Rev. George Ornsby (Surtees Society, 1868).

[2] John Cosin was born at Norwich on S. Andrew's Day, 1595. Overall—to whom the Church of England owes a debt of gratitude to this hour for the priceless boon which he bequeathed to her in the dogmatic teaching upon the Sacraments, in the Church Catechism, and also for the influence of his theological teaching, which in no small degree was effectual in saving the Church from the narrow, unscriptural, Calvinistic spirit set forth in the Lambeth Articles—was Regius Professor of Divinity at Cambridge in Cosin's undergraduate days. To Dr. Overall, successively Bishop of Lichfield and Norwich, Cosin became secretary and librarian. In February, 1635, Cosin was elected Master of Peterhouse in succession to Dr. Matthew Wren, then promoted to the See of Hereford, who after the Restoration became Bishop of Ely. In 1640 Cosin was Vice-Chancellor of the University, but was ejected from his mastership in 1643. He was deprived of his other preferments, and

Summary and Conclusion. 153

Sparrow may have seen these *Considerations*, together with the *Notes upon the Common Prayer*, wherein, in the *Third Series*, probably written before 1640, Cosin cites the rubrics from the Order in the second year of King Edward VI., both for communicating the sick with the reserved Sacrament, and also for celebrating in the sick man's house if there were no open Communion in the Church. Adding:—

"And of all this Order (even as it was in the second year of King Edward) Bucer gave his censure, That it was altogether agreeable to the word of God" (*vide supra*, p. 16).

withdrew to Paris, where, by order from King Charles, he officiated as Chaplain in the English Ambassador's Chapel, where Divine Service, according to the Anglican rite, was celebrated with much dignity. Cosin, after living in exile seventeen years—during which he suffered much privation—was consecrated Bishop of Durham on December 2nd, 1660. He took the leading part in the Revision of the Prayer Book in 1661. *Obdormivit in Xto*, Jan. 15th, 1672, within half an hour of receiving the *Viaticum;* and the last word he said was "Lord." (*Cf.* Introduction to *Bishop Cosin's Correspondence*, vols. I. and II.)

Anthony Sparrow was born in Suffolk, and educated at Queens' College, Cambridge, where he was Scholar and afterwards Fellow. In 1643, like Cosin, he was ejected on account of his loyalty to King Charles. In 1657, "when the enemies of the Church were triumphant," he published his *Rationale* upon the Book of Common Prayer. In 1662 he was elected to the Mastership of Queens' College. November 3rd, 1667, he was consecrated Bishop of Exeter; in 1676 he was translated to the See of Norwich, where he died in 1688. Besides the *Rationale*, Bishop Sparrow also published a collection of Articles, Canons, etc., of the later English Church, a *Caution against False Doctrine*, in a charge to the Diocese of Exeter at his Primary Visitation, and a remarkable sermon upon *Confession of Sins and the Power of Absolution*, preached before the University of Cambridge in 1637. *Cf.* Editor's Preface by "J. H. N., Oriel College, Sept. 6th, 1839," prefixed to reprint of *Rationale*, by John Henry Parker (Oxford, 1843).

Thus it is not surprising to find Sparrow also referring to the Book of 1549, by way of supplying omissions in the then existing Order.

(v) Hence we gather that the question of Reservation for the sick was distinctly present to the minds of the Revisers in 1661; the Order of 1549 was certainly before them, in which, as Sparrow had so recently set forth in his *Rationale*, it is provided in the first place:—

"If the same day (that the sick is to receive the Communion) there be a Celebration of the holy Communion in the Church, then shall the Priest reserve (at the open Communion) so much of the Sacrament of the Body and Blood as shall serve the sick person, and so many as shall communicate with him. And as soon as he may conveniently, after the open Communion ended in the Church, shall go and minister the same first to them that are appointed to communicate with the sick, if there be any, and last of all to the sick."

And secondly:—

"But if the day wherein the sick person is to receive Communion, be not appointed for the open Communion in the Church; then upon convenient warning given, the Curate shall come and visit the sick person afore noon. And cutting off the form of visitation at the Psalm, *In Thee, O Lord*, shall go straight to the Communion."[1]

For the reasons already given, it was not then judged advisable to restore the rubrics which explicitly directed the practice of Reservation, in the Book of 1549; accordingly the Revisers confined

---

[1] *Cf. Rationale upon the Book of Common Prayer.* "By Anth. Sparrow, D.D., now Lord Bishop of *Exon*" (London, 1668), pp. 349, 350.

themselves to correcting the rubrics in the then existing form; these corrections, it is to be observed, being taken substantially from the Order provided in 1549 for *The Celebration of the Holy Communion for the Sick*, without one word of censure respecting the traditional usage in times past of reserving the holy Sacrament. In both these respects the Revisers were wonderfully guided in following ancient precedents; inasmuch as there were no explicit directions, in the ancient Offices of the Church of England, to reserve the Eucharist for the sick (*vide supra*, Chap. IV. 3); while on the other hand, there is distinct authority for the private celebration (where all things necessary for the same are so prepared that the Priest may reverently minister), as recorded, in similar instances, of S. Ambrose and other of the Fathers,[1] also as referred to by the Ven. Bede, and as suggested by the Mass for the sick provided in mediæval times.

(vi) But while the Revisers thus improved the Order for the private Celebration for the sick, they omitted to "set down how much of the Communion Service shall be used"— "*If the same day (that the sick is to receive the Communion) there be a celebration of the holy Communion in the Church.*" In this case therefore, as Bishop Sparrow observes, our present Order "seems to refer us to former directions in

---

[1] *Cf.* Pellicia, *Polity of the Christian Church*, edited by Rev. J. C. Bellett, p. 225.

times past." Accordingly it is not surprising that the venerable author here made no alterations in his *Rationale*, since no *substantial* change had been adopted in this respect at the Revision in 1661; and evidently "*the alterations were made*," as stated in the Preface, "*for the better direction of them that are to officiate*." His reference "to former directions in times past" is therefore still needed; while the significant way in which he directs attention to this point in the Table of Contents, thus, "How much of the Communion Service shall be used at the delivery of the Communion to the sick, *in case there had that day been a Communion*," clearly indicates a distinct omission in our present Order, except so far as it emphasises our contention that inasmuch as the Reservation of the Eucharist rests primarily upon primitive (if not apostolic) tradition, as witnessed by the Common Law of the Universal Church—the *jura non scripta* of the Spiritualty—subsequently regulated and enjoined by the Canon Law, it is not necessary that it should be specified in the rubrics; and that in this respect there is a remarkable agreement between our present form and the venerable monuments of antiquity.

(vii) Thus it is sufficient to observe, in answer to the objection that this passage in the *Rationale* does not apply to our present Order as revised in 1661:—First, that the general scope of the alterations then made is set forth in the Preface then prefixed to the Book of Common Prayer; from which we learn "That most of the alterations were made . . . . *for the better direction of them that are to officiate in any part of Divine Service*"; a statement which entirely covers the rubrical directions then made in this Order for the Communion of the Sick. Moreover, that it is obviously impossible to suppose that any substantial alteration, such as that involved in forbidding the primitive and Catholic usage of reserving the Eucharist for the sick and dying, could even have been contemplated, in the face of the statement of the Revisers themselves that they had "rejected all such [alterations] as were . . . . of dangerous consequence, *as secretly striking at some established doctrine or laudable practice of the Church of England, or indeed of the whole Catholic Church of Christ.*"

And secondly, we must remember that, in the latter part of the seventeenth century, the *Rationale* was no obscure or obsolete book, such as it has now unhappily become, in consequence of having been superseded (through the changed temper of the times) by works of a less edifying and patristic character; but on the contrary, that it was the most popular devotional commentary on the Book of Common Prayer during the fifty or sixty years which followed the Restoration, as is evident from the numerous editions which were then called for. Several editions of the *Rationale* were issued during the author's life-time, and by his authority, "in which," as Dr. Newman observes, "he did not think it necessary to alter the rubrics and collects as they stood when it was first published, according to the revised Prayer Book put forth by authority of Convocation in 1661"; probably because in these respects there was no substantial alteration made by that revision. But if it had been intended to prohibit Reservation for the sick by the sixth Postcommunion rubric (then inserted), and by the rubrical corrections then made in the Order for the Communion of the Sick, is it reasonable to suppose that one of the Revisers could have publicly maintained, and this on repeated occasions,—more particularly by the re-issue of the *Rationale* in 1668, just after his elevation to the Episcopate in November 1667, and again in 1676 upon his translation to the See of Norwich, as though speaking with authority as a father in Christ,—that in his opinion the practice of Reservation was still to be commended as being agreeable to the ancient usage of this Church and Realm? Is it conceivable, if Reservation had really been forbidden, that other bishops would have made no remonstrance when the then recent prohibition was thus publicly ignored? Moreover, if this were so, how could Bishop Sparrow himself, as charged to maintain discipline within his diocese, have left this passage without correction, since otherwise it might at any

Summary and Conclusion. 159

time become an occasion of disobedience and of scandal to the clergy and laity of his jurisdiction?

(viii) It may indeed be suggested that this (like other passages) was left as originally published, *per incuriam*. This, however, is negatived by the fact that, in other respects, important alterations were made in the several editions of the *Rationale*, by way of omission and addition. Thus in the edition of 1668, the very important passage beginning *This Sacrament should be received fasting*, which sets forth, explains, and commends the primitive usage of fasting Communion, is added as an appendix, whereas in 1676 and all subsequent editions it is incorporated in its proper place in the commentary upon Holy Communion. Again, in 1668 Bishop Andrewes' *Form of Consecration of a Church or Chappel*, etc. is added, as though intended for use in the Diocese of *Exon;* while in 1676 its place is taken by the Bishop of *Exon's Caution against False Doctrine*, in a sermon at his Primary Visitation. In this edition extracts from the Acts of Parliament directing the religious observance of November 5th, of the martyrdom of King Charles I., and the Restoration of King Charles II. are appended. And in 1684 Bishop Sparrow added a valuable "*Table of Texts of Scripture*, referred to or explained, for the illustration and vindication of our Church Liturgy."

(ix) Before taking leave of Bishop Sparrow, we

may note that in his *Rationale* we find further indication of the true meaning of the sixth Post-communion rubric; in his commentary upon that rubric as it stood in the Book of 1559:—*If any of the bread and wine remain, the Curate shall have it to his own use;* wherein he explains:—

"That is, if it were not consecrated; *for if it be consecrated, it is all to be spent with fear and reverence by the communicants in the Church.*"[1]

This explanation, it must be observed, which dates from 1657, is evidently in substantial agreement with our present rubric of 1661, and virtually directs that *if any remain of that which was consecrated, it shall not be carried out of the Church, etc.*

This latter, it is argued, obviously forbids Reservation, because it is ordered that *if any remain . . . it shall* NOT *be carried out of the Church:* just as the author of the *Rationale* here enjoins, that *it is* ALL *to be spent with fear and reverence . . . in the Church.*

But, as we have already seen, Bishop Sparrow directs in accordance with ancient usage, when commenting upon the Communion of the sick, that if occasion so require, "*the Priest* SHALL RESERVE *(at the open Communion) so much of the Sacrament of the Body and Blood as shall serve the sick person*, and so many as shall communicate with him."[2]

---

[1] *Cf. Rationale*, ed. 1668, p. 279.
[2] *Ibid.* p. 349.

Clearly therefore this direction—that, *if any remain of that which was consecrated "it is all to be spent with fear and reverence in the Church"*; or, in the words of the rubric, "*it shall not be carried out of the Church*"—cannot, if historical considerations are of any value, and rubrics are to be consistently interpreted, be intended to refer to "so much of the Sacrament" as might be needed for the Communion of the sick, which the Priest is here directed previously to "*Reserve.*"

Nor is there any real discrepancy between this "former direction" to reserve and the present rubric, which virtually enjoins that all which may not be so required shall be "reverently" consumed.

"Every Sunday at the least," according to the Ecclesiastical Law, the priest is directed to reserve so much as may be required for the Communion of the sick, and then "if any remain of that which was consecrated"—*Hostias, si quæ fuerint remanentes*—(as in Lyndwood's gloss), "the Priest," either with his Ministers,—*a Sacerdote, et ejus ministris, videlicet Diacono et Subdiacono,*—or "and such other of the Communicants as he shall then call unto him, shall immediately after the Blessing," that is, "in the Church before all the people depart from it" (as in Cosin's *Considerations, vide supra*), "with fear and reverence" (as here directed in the *Rationale*), receive and consume the same,—*recipi et consumi* (*Provinciale*).

Upon all other occasions, save when the needs of

162   *Reservation of the Blessed Sacrament.*

the sick so require,—*Nam et aliis diebus innovari potest, instante necessitate; quia Presbyter semper habebit Eucharistiam paratam propter infirmantes.* (*Lyndw.*)—the Priest, "immediately after the Blessing," will proceed to unveil "what remaineth of the consecrated Elements,"—*i.e. pars reservata usque in finem Missæ, secundum antiquum ecclesiæ Romanæ morem* (*vide supra*),—and (if need be) with his Ministers, "or other of the Communicants," will then "reverently eat and drink the same."

5.

Concerning the Latin Prayer-book of 1560.

Before concluding this Treatise, it seems desirable to add the following considerations respecting the authority of the Latin Prayer-book of 1560, already referred to in support of the traditional usage of reserving the Blessed Sacrament for the sick, as co-existing with the appointed Order for the Communion of the Sick, under the *English* Prayer-book of 1559.

(i) In order adequately to estimate the authority of the Latin Prayer-book of 1560, in its reference to this question, it is necessary to bear in mind the condition of ecclesiastical affairs at the accession of Elizabeth; when a state of things prevailed, which (though not confined to that particular epoch) was, in a greater or less degree, specially characteristic of the sixteenth century. The condition here referred to is the very remarkable intrusion, which we observe, on the part of the Temporalty in the conduct or control of Spiritual matters; in short, in the supremacy of that Erastian spirit, in its most aggravated form, which hesitated not to "give unto Cæsar the things that be God's." Such was the temper which predominated throughout the Reformation period. It is not surprising, therefore, that much was done in virtue of the Royal prerogative, or by authority of Parliament, which in a normal condition of secular and ecclesiastical life, would have been inaugurated and concluded by the Spiritualty, with the concurrence and sanction of the legitimate authority of Temporal princes and of Christian states. But in the sixteenth century constitutional authority was practically unknown. Among the conflicting forces which contributed to this result, none were more powerful than the unconstitutional encroachments of the Papacy. From the time of Hildebrand onward, aided by the forged Decretals, which (as Bishop Forbes observes) "were framed not by Rome, nor with its cognizance, but as a protection against lawless civil power";[1] the divinely ordained πρωτέια, or primacy of the Apostolic See, together with that pre-eminence (πρεσβέια) accorded by early Councils to the Bishop of Rome, had been overlaid by an usurped supremacy, which claimed to exercise an universal lordship over all things human and divine.[2]

---

[1] *Cf. Explanation of the Thirty-Nine Articles*, Art. xxxvii. p. 741.

[2] "Flatterers, on public occasions too, called the Pope 'another

The result of this intrusion on the part of man into the Headship of Christ, combined with the temporal sovereignty assumed by the Pope, was twofold. In the first place, it provoked a determined opposition in England both on the part of Church and State:—"Long before the Reformation," says Bishop Forbes, "there was a strong anti-Italian party in the English Church, and it must never be forgotten that the actual breach was consummated by the Catholic Convocation of the Church, by Gardiner, and Bonner, and Warham."[1] Among the laity, this same spirit of resistance had already found legal expression in the Statutes of *Præmunire*, passed in 27 Edw. III. and in 16 Rich. II.[2] In the next place the ecclesiastical jurisdiction was weakened and laid prostrate by the uncanonical action of a foreign Prelate (1) in encouraging appeals from the Diocesan and Provincial Courts; (2) in superseding the ancient method of confirming the election of bishops and metropolitans; (3) by the intrusion of non-resident foreigners, for the most part prelates or dependents of the Papal Court, into the episcopal sees and benefices of England.

(ii) It is no wonder therefore that, under a

God upon earth.' *Tu denique alter Deus in terris*, said to Julius II. *in Lat. Conc.*, Sess. IV., Dec. 10th, 1512."

"Alexander VI. dispensed with what was, or was hitherto accounted to be, Divine law." *Cf.* Bp. Forbes on the Articles, p. 747.

[1] Bp. Forbes, *Explanation of the Thirty-Nine Articles*, p. 741.
[2] *Ibid.* p. 751.

Summary and Conclusion. 165

sovereign like Henry VIII., the rejection of the usurped authority of the Roman Curia was really undertaken by the king and enacted by parliament, though ratified by the clergy in the Convocations of both provinces. This precedent was followed in the reign of Edward VI. in authorising the English Service, and in making other ecclesiastical changes. Upon the accession of Mary the same course was adopted in repealing Edward's Act of Uniformity, and in replacing the Latin Service, used in the last year of the reign of King Henry VIII.[1] In like manner the English Service, as used in the latter part of the reign of Edward VI., though with certain significant alterations, was restored by the joint authority of the Queen and Parliament in the first year of the reign of Elizabeth. It is to be observed that the Book of Common Prayer of 1559,

[1] From the following section from Mary's *Act for the Repeal of certain Statutes, etc.*, it is plain that the Latin Service was enjoined by authority of Parliament, just as the English Service had been authorised in the reign of Edward VI. :—

"III. And be it further enacted by the Authoritie aforesaid, That all such Divine Service and Administration of Sacraments, as were most commonly used in the Realme of England in the last Yeere of the Reigne of our late Sovereigne Lord King *Henrie* the Eight, shall be, from and after the Twentieth Day of *December*, in this present yeere of our Lord God 1553, used and frequented through the whole Realme of England, and all other the Queenes Majesties Dominions. And that no kind nor Order of Divine Service, nor Administration of Sacraments, be after the sayd Twentieth Day of *December* used, or ministered in any other maner, forme or degree, within the said Realme of England, or other the Queenes Dominions, than was most commonly used and frequented in the sayd last yeere of the Reigne of the sayd late King *Henrie* the Eight." 1 *Mar.* Sess. II. Cap. 2.

so far as it differed from the ancient service-books of the Church of England, rested solely and exclusively upon secular authority, and that the Queen insisted upon certain alterations, such as the use of the Eucharistic vestments and ancient *Ornamenta,* the altar-wise position of the Lord's Table, the use of wafer-bread, and of the time-honoured formula of administration; moreover, that the Communion should be received kneeling, notwithstanding the wishes of the ultra-reforming party; and that the Declaration upon this matter, apparently denying "any real or essential presence there being of Christ's natural flesh and blood," added to the Communion Office by royal authority in 1552, should be entirely omitted. In all these respects, therefore, the usage of the second year of Edward VI. was advisedly restored, concurrently with the adoption of his second Book, thus brought into conformity with the Order prescribed under the Book of 1549. No reference whatever was made to Convocation, just as no reference was made thereto when the Latin Service was restored after the accession of Mary; indeed, as Cardwell remarks, "to have referred the whole question to the Convocations of the two provinces would have been to put an end to the progress of the Reformation."[1]

So likewise with the Latin Prayer Book, authorised by Royal Letters Patent in 1560, which was

---

[1] *Cf. History of Conferences, etc.,* p. 20 (Oxford, 1849).

Summary and Conclusion. 167

evidently designed to recognise and bring back more completely the usages of 1549, concurrently with the use of the English Book of 1559. No doubt the Latin Service was primarily intended for the use of Clergy who were living in Colleges or ministering in Collegiate Churches; this is plain from the Letters Patent authorising its use, and also that it was issued at their request. But it was also commended to all the English clergy :—

"Eadem etiam formula Latina precandi privatim uti hortamur omnes reliquos Ecclesiæ nostræ Anglicanæ ministros, cujuscumque gradus fuerint, iis diebus, quibus aut non solent, aut non tenentur parochianis suis, ad ædem sacram pro more accedentibus, publice preces vernacula lingua, secundum formam dicti Statuti, recitare."[1]

(iii) It is also important to observe that the use of this Latin Service was one of the subjects included in the "further order" which the Queen was authorised to take under the Act of Uniformity of 1559, "with the advice of her commissioners for causes ecclesiastical or of the Metropolitan of this Realm." Accordingly we find Elizabeth thus writing to her commissioners,—the Archbishop of Canterbury, the Bishop of London, Dr. Byll, the Queen's Almoner, then Dean of Westminster, and Walter Haddon, who had been chiefly engaged in revising and preparing the Latin version of the Prayer-book,—under date of January 22nd, 1561:—

[1] *Cf. Liturgical Services set forth in the reign of Queen Elizabeth* (Parker Society), p. 302. Cardwell, *Documentary Annals, etc.*, I. 281.

"Letting you to understande, that where it is provided by acte of parliament, holden in the first yere of our reigne, that whensoever we shall see cause to take further order in any rite or ceremonie, appointed in the Book of Common Prayer, and our pleasure knowne therein, either to our commissioners for causes ecclesiasticall, or to the metropolitane, that then eftsoones consideration should be had therein."

In this "further order" the Queen directs her commissioners:—"to peruse the Order of the said lessons throughout the whole year, *and to cause some new Kalendars to be imprinted*,[1] whereby such chapters or parcells of less edification may be removed, and other more profitable may supply their roomes; and further also to consider, as becometh, the forsaide great disorders *in the decaies of churches and in the unseemly keepinge and order of the chauncells*, . . .

"And further, we will that, where we have caused our Book of Common Service to be translated into the Latin tongue, for the use and exercise of such studentes, *und other learned in the Latin tongue;* we will also that by your wisdome and discretions, *ye prescribe some good orders to the collegiate churches*, to which we have permitted the use of the divine service and prayer in Latin tongue, in such sorte as ye shall consider to be most mete to be used, in respect of their companies, *or of resorte of our laye subjectes to the said churches*, so that our good

---

[1] In consequence of this "further order" the black-letter holidays were for the most part added to the Kalendar from the Latin Prayer-book of 1560.

purpose in the said translation be not frustrated, nor be corruptlie abused, contrarie to the effect of our meaning."[1]

Thus we find that although the Latin translation here referred to was not prepared until after the Act of 1559, its use in Collegiate Churches was regulated under the aforesaid provision of that Act, and that herein it was regarded as having co-ordinate authority with the English Book of Common Prayer.

In this Latin version, which was in substantial agreement with the English Prayer-book, and was thus commended by authority to all the Clergy of the Realm, the traditional usage of Reservation for the sick was distinctly recognised and enjoined. This Book, moreover, was generally accepted by the Clergy, particularly in "collegiate churches," as is plain from the above "order," under the Act of Uniformity, that the Metropolitan and other Commissioners should "prescribe some good orders" for "the use of the divine service and prayer in Latin tongue."

"The Marian clergy," says Bishop Forbes, "were not exterminated; they conformed, partly in hope of better times, partly from fear of the Government, partly moved by a sincere desire for Reformation; but still, the traditions of a whole life-time

---

[1] *Cf. Documentary Annals*, LV. vol. I. 295—297. Bp. Gibson's *Codex*, I. 309 n., 319 n.

cannot be destroyed in a moment, and any great shock to their feelings would have led them to act as the eighty rectors, fifty prebendaries, fifteen masters of colleges, twelve archdeacons, twelve deans, and six abbots and abbesses, actually did, that is, abandon their preferments. We are left to the dilemma that either the great mass of the lower clergy were a set of unprincipled self-seekers, or that the changes, interpreted by custom and previous usage, were so small that no real violence was done to their consciences." [1]

If we place ourselves in the position of the great body of the clergy of that period, who had been accustomed to the traditional usage of reserving the Eucharist for the sick, as enjoined in the Ecclesiastical Law, though not prescribed by the Sarum and York manuals, with an English Service-book put into their hands, in which this same usage was likewise not prescribed, though it was nowhere forbidden,—but with a Latin Office-book of like authority, commended to their use, in which the traditional usage was enjoined,—is it possible to come to any other conclusion than this:—that the practice of Reservation would be continued as a matter of course, and in fact was so intended to be observed? How could the same priest, designated

[1] *Cf.* Bp. Forbes on the *Articles, Epistle Dedicatory*, XXIX. in which the reader will find a most interesting and instructive *résumé* of the course of events which determined the condition of ecclesiastical affairs in England upon the accession of Elizabeth.

Summary and Conclusion. 171

as "Curate" in the English form, and as *Parochus* in the Latin *Communio Infirmorum*, possibly conclude, or be intended to conclude, that the traditional usage, authorised in the one case, was unlawful in the other? Is it not a *reductio ad absurdum* gravely to maintain that while the parish priest was perfectly justified in reserving the Sacrament for the Communion of sick members of colleges within his parish, he must on no account do so for any other parishioners whatsoever?

(iv) It is of course admitted that, strictly speaking, the Latin Prayer-book of 1560 was technically without ecclesiastical authorisation; that defect, however, has already been accounted for by the exceptional crisis through which the Church was then passing; while on the other hand, it must in fairness be allowed that the same objection applies with equal force to the English Prayer-book of 1559; both of which were accepted by the clergy as being in substantial agreement with the older forms and offices of the Church; and also, that the Latin Book was issued with all the authorisation and warrant which was then possible. Its gradual disuse during the latter part of Elizabeth's reign was due to the growing spirit of Puritanism, particularly in the two Universities, which caused a wide-spread dissidence among the clergy from the Catholic standard of faith and practice. It is, however, interesting to note, as one of the many indications of restored Church life and feeling in the reign of Charles I., that in the Convocation of 1640 the Archbishop proposed, "that his Majesty might be moved for the new printing of the Book of Common Prayer in the Latin tongue, alleging the rubric in which it is provided that *when men say Morning and Evening Prayer privately, they may say the same in any language that they themselves do understand.*" [1]

This proposal is thus referred to in the *Acts and Proceedings of Convocation*, in the official report of the *Ultima Sessio* of the memorable Convocation of 1640 :—

"Et Reverendissimus cum unanimi consensu prælatorum et cleri hujus sacræ Synodi decrevit regiam Majestatem supplicandam fore, ut *Liber Publicarum Precum*, in Latinum versus, *reimprimatur* prout in actu synodico sequenti continetur, viz. 'Decernimus insuper,' etc." [2]

Thus we learn that the Archbishop, "with the unanimous consent of the Bishops and Clergy of this sacred Synod, decreed that the King's Majesty should be moved *for the new printing* of the *Liber Publicarum Precum*"; presumably that which had been originally issued by royal authority in 1560, the use of none other having been regulated under the Act of Uniformity. The times, however, were not favourable for the completion of this and other measures then designed for God's glory and the

[1] *Cf.* Cardwell's *Synodalia*, vol. II. 596.
[2] *Ibid.* xxx. p. 628.

welfare of His Church. There is a touching interest attaching to this *Ultima Sessio* of the Convocation of 1640; it was the last occasion upon which the venerable Primate, Laud, presided over the Convocation of his province. We read in the *Acta*:—

"Reverendissimus Pater, ob honorem et reverentiam dicti domini nostri Regis juxta tenorem brevis Regii prædicti, eandem Convocationem sive Sacram Synodum Provincialem dissolvit."[1]

(v) Before the Convocation again met at S. Paul's, May 8th, 1661, the Church in this land had indeed passed through the very furnace of affliction; Archbishop Laud and his royal master, King Charles the First, had both witnessed a good confession in defence of the faith and liberties of the Kingdom of God. But "the blood of Martyrs is the seed of the Church"; in the martyrdom of the Supreme Ruler of the State and of the chief Pastor of the Church, and in the subsequent overthrow both of royal and ecclesiastical authority, which the encroachments of the Papacy in bygone years, and of the Temporal power in more recent times, had generated, the *pœna peccati*—the penalty of the sins of the fathers—had been paid. In the Restoration of the Monarchy and of the Church we note the triumph of constitutional authority, and of that supernatural energy, which is the very life of the Church of God. Accordingly, in the Convocation

[1] Cardwell's *Synodalia*, vol. II. p. 630.

of 1661, it was again practically recognised, as set forth by the Convocation of 1559 :—

"That the authority of handling and defining concerning the things belonging to faith, sacraments, and discipline ecclesiastical, hath hitherto ever belonged and ought to belong only to the pastors of the Church; whom the Holy Ghost for this purpose hath set in the Church; and not to laymen."[1]

This fundamental principle was emphasised and set forth in the revision and promulgation of the *Book of Common Prayer* by the Spiritualty, with the concurrence and legislative sanction of the Temporalty. Accordingly we read that, in Session XLVIII. of the Convocation of 1661, the revised *Book of Common Prayer*, with the *Form and Manner of Making, Ordaining, and Consecrating Bishops, Priests and Deacons*, "having been first received, approved, and subscribed by the Most Reverend Lord and Father in Christ, William, by Divine providence Lord Archbishop of Canterbury, Primate of all England and Metropolitan" :—

"Dicti Episcopi ejusdem provinciæ in Sacra provinciali Synodo legitime congregati, unanimi assensu et consensu in formam redegerunt, receperunt, et approbarunt, eisdemque subscripserunt. Et postea omnes episcopi prædicti tunc præsen' et congregat', exceptis reverendis patribus dominis Oxon', Asaphen',

---

[1] *Cf.* Cardwell's *History of Conferences, etc.*, p. 23. The following is the original *Articulus cleri* from the *Acta* of Convocation in the first year of Elizabeth:—"Item. Quod auctoritas tractandi et definiendi de iis, quæ spectant ad fidem, sacramenta, et disciplinam ecclesiasticam, hactenus semper spectavit, et spectare debet tantum ad pastores ecclesiæ, quos Spiritus S. in hoc in ecclesiæ Dei posuit, et non ad laicos."— *Synodalia*, II. 493.

et Laudaven' episcopis, ad domum parliamenti sese contulerunt, et dictos respective episcopos in dicta domo convocationis reliquerunt ad videndum clerum inferioris domus convocationis dicto libro subscribere; dictoque clero unanimi consensu subscribente idem reverendus pater Robertus Oxon' episcopus, etc., continuavit, etc., juxta schedulam, etc."[1]

In this eventful Convocation (so important in its far-reaching consequences, not only to the Church of England but, it may be, to "the whole Catholic Church of Christ") the present English rite was first revised, approved, and promulgated with full spiritual authority, and thus became binding *in foro conscientiæ* upon all whom God has placed within the canonical jurisdiction of His Church in this land; save those who, through no fault of their own it may be, are unhappily, though not wilfully, estranged from Catholic Communion. In this Convocation likewise the review of the Latin Prayer Book was not neglected.

(vi) Accordingly, in Session LXXX. of this same Convocation, under date of April 26th, 1662, we read in the official *Acta :*—

"Et tractatu inter eos habit' et fact' de translatione Libri Publicarum Precum in sermonem Latinum, dominus episcopus London. etc., de et cum consensu confratrum suorum, etc. Curam translationis ejusdem reverendis viris Johanni Earle decano B. Petri Westm' et Johanni Peirson sacræ respective theologiæ professoribus commisit."[2]

---

[1] *Cf.* Cardwell's *Synodalia*, vol. II. xxxi. p. 660.

[2] *Cf. Ibid.* vol. II. 671. Dr. Peirson, the learned author of the *Exposition of the Creed*, was then Archdeacon of Surrey, and afterwards Bishop of Chester.

Upon comparing this Act of Convocation respecting the Latin Prayer-book with that of 1640, it is to be observed that, whereas this latter "with the unanimous consent of the bishops and clergy ... decreed that the King's Majesty might be moved for the *new printing* of the *Liber Publicarum Precum,*" the Act of 1662 contemplated a *new translation* of the same.

In Session CXXV. upon May 18th, 1662, "this Latin version of the Common Prayer, having been brought in, was referred to the care and revision of the Reverend Father in Christ, John, by Divine permission Bishop of Sarum, and of John Dolben, S.T.P., Dean of Westminster." But there is no record of any further action with regard to this matter.[1]

Nevertheless, it is provided by the Act of Uniformity of that same year, which gave statutory force to the Book of Common Prayer:—

"That it shall and may be lawful to use the Morning and Evening Prayer, and all other Prayers and Services prescribed in and by the said Book, in the Chapels, or other public places of the respective Colleges and Halls in both the Universities, in the

---

[1] Cardwell's *Synodalia*, vol. II. p. 683. It is hoped that this revised version of the *Liber Precum Publicarum* may be preserved among the Records of Convocation, and may eventually be published. Such a document could not fail to be instructive, as indicating the mind of the Revisers respecting several points of interest; more especially as being in part the work of that accomplished divine and patristic scholar, *The most excellent Bishop Peirson, the very dust of whose writings is gold.*

Colleges of Westminster, Winchester, and Eton, and in the Convocations of the Clergy of either Province, in Latin; anything in this Act to the contrary notwithstanding."

But, as we have just seen, the proposed Latin version having been referred to the Bishop of Salisbury and Dean of Westminster for further revision, was never received nor adopted by Convocation. We are therefore thrown back upon the former Latin version, published originally by royal authority in 1560, but possessed of statutory force under the former Act of Uniformity of 1559, as being included in the "other order" which the Queen was therein authorised to take "with the advice of her Commissioners appointed and authorised under the Great Seal of England for causes Ecclesiastical, or of the Metropolitan of this Realm." In each and all of which particulars the method of procedure regulating the use of the Latin Prayer-book was in conformity with the requirements of the aforesaid Statute. Thus Bishop Gibson observes upon the provision for the Latin Service, in the clause of the Act of Uniformity of 1662, above quoted, that:—

"Although no provision was made for this liberty in the foregoing Act of Eliz. I. c. 2, yet the Queen, by her Letters Patent, bearing date April 6, 1560, granted it (*nostra aucthoritate et privilegio Regali*) to the Colleges of the two Universities, and to those of Winchester and Eton. But afterwards (*Anno Regni* 3°) the Archbishop, Bishop of London, Dr. Bill, and Dr. Haddon, were commissioned (among other things) to limit the use of that liberty in *Collegiate Churches*, with regard to those of the laity who resorted thither."[1]

[1] *Cf.* Bp. Gibson's *Codex*, I. p. 319 n.

This Commission had been previously referred to by Bishop Gibson as granted under the clause of the Act of 1559, providing that:—

"The Queen's Majesty may, by the like advice of the said Commissioners or Metropolitan, ordain and publish such *further Ceremonies or Rites* as may be most for the advancement of God's Glory, the edifying of His Church, and due reverence of Christ's holy Mysteries and Sacraments." [1]

And we have also seen that this Latin Prayer-book of 1560, as the only Latin version possessed of co-ordinate authority with the English Book of Common Prayer, received the unanimous assent of the bishops and clergy in the sacred Synod of 1640, in their decree that the King's Majesty should be moved for the new printing of the same. Thus the original defect in the authorisation of the *Liber Precum Publicarum* was virtually rectified, and the said book still remains the only Latin version of the English Prayer-book which is sanctioned by royal, statutory, and synodical authority; although it still needs the revision contemplated in the Convocation of 1662, to bring it into more exact agreement with the revised Book of Common Prayer.[2]

---

[1] *Cf.* Bp. Gibson's *Codex*, I. p. 309.

[2] The author desires to guard against the appearance of derogating from the acknowledged excellence of the Latin version of the *Book of Common Prayer*, edited by the Rev. Dr. Bright, Canon of Christ Church, Regius Professor of Ecclesiastical History in the University of Oxford, and the Rev. P. G. Medd, Hon. Canon of S. Albans, sometime Senior Fellow of University College. After constantly using this edition of the *Liber Precum Publicarum* since its publication in 1865,

Summary and Conclusion. 179

(vii) The author has felt it desirable thus to state at length the historical evidence, from public records, touching the *Liber Precum* of 1560 for the following reasons :—

First,—because, in estimating its bearing upon the question of reserving the Eucharist for the sick, it is necessary that we should see clearly, by the light of historical considerations and from public documents, what is the precise nature of its evidential value and authorisation.

Secondly,—because, so far as the author is aware, the above evidence has never before been brought together in a connected chain of argument; consequently, as he ventures to think, it has been too hastily concluded (*a*) that the *Liber Precum* of 1560 rests exclusively upon royal authority, and (*b*) that it has been entirely superseded by the Act of Uniformity of 1662; whereas, as the documentary

the writer would cordially commend it to his brethren of the clergy as a valuable aid in the fulfilment of a primary obligation; and further, as fostering the ecclesiastical spirit, in maintaining a knowledge of the Latin tongue and affording a deeper insight into the meaning of the English Office. Nevertheless, valuable as this version undoubtedly is, it lacks the *imprimatur* of authority and of synodical recognition which belongs to the *Liber Precum* of 1560, and which gives special weight and significance to its witness to the continuance of the primitive usage of reserving the Eucharist for the sick, under the Reformed Order of the Church of England.

In compiling the Oxford version of 1865, the Latin Book of 1560 has not been neglected, but it is suggested that the Offices provided in this Book for (1) the *Communio Infirmorum*, (2) *In Commendationibus Benefactorum*, (3) the *Celebratio Cænæ Domini in Funebribus*, would be a valuable addition to the Appendix.

evidence testifies, it still continues to be the only Latin version of the Book of Common Prayer which, in addition to its publication by Royal Letters Patent in 1560, acquired statutory force under the Act of 1559 by the "further order" of the Queen, with the advice of her commissioners, as expressly provided in that Statute; and that, like the *Revised Table of Lessons*, issued under the same "order," it is, strictly speaking, part of the Queen's Ecclesiastical Law, as a "*further Rite*" authorised by the Act of 1559, clause XXVI.

Thirdly,—because, in addition to the informal sanction of the Spiritualty, testified by the original acceptance of the *Liber Precum* by the clergy, its use was expressly contemplated and sanctioned by the Provincial Synod of Canterbury in 1640; whereof the *Acts and Proceedings* were approved by the Convocation of York, and confirmed under the Great Seal.[1]

Finally,—because, notwithstanding its manifold defects in falling far short of being an adequate version of the present English Rite, nevertheless, upon historical and liturgical grounds, it must be regarded as an illustrative document of great value, which cannot be ignored in estimating the scope and bearing of the rubrical corrections made in the Convocation of 1661.

Hence, in interpreting (1) the sixth Post-com-

[1] *Cf. Synodalia*, II. pp. 628, 597.

munion rubric, (2) the prescribed Order for the Communion of the Sick, (3) the Twenty-eighth Article of 1562, which was re-made by the very clergy who had accepted the Latin Prayer-book of 1560, it must be remembered that in this *Liber Precum Publicarum* the primitive usage of reserving the Eucharist for the sick is distinctly authorised; moreover, that the said Book is of co-ordinate authority with the English Book of Common Prayer, because its use was duly regulated under the Act of Uniformity in 1561; and that, until further action herein is taken by Convocation and sanctioned by the Crown, this particular recognition of the Reservation of the Blessed Sacrament for the Communion of the sick still holds good, under the established Order of this Church and Realm.

6.

The author is not unmindful of the responsibility of traversing the Report of a Committee of Convocation in which this Tractate originated, and of virtually suggesting that it may eventually be re-considered, or at least may not be pressed; but he has consented at the request of friends—both of the clergy and among medical men—to direct attention to the Anglican authority, and practical necessity, for the Reservation of the Eucharist for the sick. Some requests there are which have the imperative nature of commands; so it has been in

Conclusion.

this present instance. This task, he knows full well, has been very inadequately fulfilled, but it has been rendered lighter by the following considerations, which have encouraged him in thus venturing to invite public attention to this momentous subject.

(i) The statement of his Grace the Primate in his Diocesan Conference last summer, to the effect that the Report in question was not to be regarded as representing the Upper House of Convocation, because it was in fact the Report of a Committee, brought a sense of relief to the minds of many Churchmen, with the hope of a fair and kindly desire in high quarters to do justice to this matter.[1]

Likewise the statement by the Bishop of Chester, when this subject was discussed in the Upper House of the York Convocation, ought not to be forgotten. His lordship, in giving a guarded assent to the Resolution, observed that:—

"So far he should be happy to support the Resolution, but he should not like to support the Resolution if it was understood to imply any sweeping condemnation of the practice which had been used throughout the whole Church for many centuries, and which was recognised as lawful in the first Prayer-book of the reformed Church, in the case which the Bishop of Newcastle had mentioned."

His Grace the President also observed that:—

---

[1] *Cf.* Report in *The Guardian*, July 7th, 1886. The author regrets that inadvertently he referred to this Resolution in Chapter II. under the impression that it was virtually a Report of the Upper House, but he gladly recognises the substantial difference in the official character of the Report, pointed out by the Archbishop.

"Of course there were certain points which would have to be thought of. Supposing we had lepers at the present moment, and those lepers were worshipping just outside the cathedral, they might not admit them into the church, but he was sure they would be willing to carry out to them the sacred Elements to enable them to join in the worship as well as if they were allowed in the church. . . . He was sure they would allow them to have Holy Communion with those in the church in the only way in which it would be then possible."[1]

(ii) The arguments advanced in support of the practice of Reservation, based upon (1) the history and intention of the formularies of the Church, referred to in Chapter II.; (2) the recognition of the principle of Reservation in the Book of Common Prayer, set forth in Chapter III.; (3) the ecclesiastical and statutory authority of the Provincial Constitutions, giving legislative force and enaction to this usage, which rests primarily upon the Common Law of the Universal Church, considered and elucidated in Chapter IV.,—will no doubt be closely questioned and, it may be, sharply criticised. Thus time will be needed in order that men's minds may become disabused of prejudice and erroneous opinions on this subject before they can accept that Catholic position of this usage in the Church of England, which historical investigation and liturgical research prove to be alone consistent with her canonical *status* as the Apostolic Communion, entitled to our allegiance in virtue of her organic unity with the Church of God throughout the world.

[1] *Cf.* Report in *The Guardian*, April 29th, 1885.

Impartial students of the Prayer-book will then find that the formularies in question have been assumed upon insufficient grounds to forbid Reservation. Liturgical scholars will perceive that all through the Service-books of the mediæval period, in the *Provinciale* and commentaries of Lyndwood, and in the English *Book of Common Prayer*, particularly when illustrated by the annotations of Hooker, Andrewes, Overall, Cosin, and Sparrow, there is, as it were, a running cypher, touching this and other matters of observance, which can only be recognised and elucidated by reference to those early liturgical writers who indicate the origin of later custom in the earliest usages of the Church of God. Those also who are learned in Ecclesiastical Law will, it is hoped, eventually allow that the ancient practice of Reservation is still enjoined in every parish church, in order that due provision for the exigencies of the sick and dying may never be omitted; and that such a Law, which does but embody and regulate the universal tradition of the Christian Church, can never be abrogated by contrary custom unless prescribed against by the custom of the whole Church.

(iii) Furthermore, it will be found, upon impartially considering the question of Communion under both kinds in its theological, historical, and practical bearings as treated in Chapter V., that this uniform tradition of the whole Church for nearly twelve

Summary and Conclusion. 185

hundred years, so happily restored in England three centuries ago, is perfectly consistent with Reservation for the sick under either kind in those cases of necessity which are expressly recognised in the Ecclesiastical Law. And therefore that the canonical rule of reserving "the Sacrament of the Body and Blood of our Lord Jesus Christ .... in a decent Tabernacle, over against the high Altar," as enjoined by Bishop Tunstall, in conformity with the Provincial Constitution (*sub Panis latibulo*), under the species of Bread, still holds good, as expressing the Ecclesiastical Law of England to be commonly observed in providing for cases of emergency; although at the same time it is perfectly legitimate, and according to ecclesiastical precedent, to reserve the holy Sacrament and to communicate the sick under both kinds in cases where "timely notice" is given and special provision can be made; and that, whenever the Eucharist is celebrated in presence of the sick, Holy Communion will be administered under both kinds, according to the public Order of the Church, saving and except in such cases of extreme necessity in which the sick person may be physically incapable of swallowing or retaining either one or the other of the consecrated Species.

Upon the whole, therefore, it is respectfully submitted that, when the force of the above line of argument is duly estimated, the suggested historical, liturgical, and canonical considerations will lead to the conclusion (1) that the Reservation of the Blessed Sacrament for the Communion of the sick and dying is in nowise inconsistent with the Order of the Church of England; (2) that the principle of Reservation is intrinsically recognised in the Book of Common Prayer; (3) that its observance is enjoined by the Ecclesiastical Law of this Realm.

Lastly, the author would express a hope that they who may not accept the conclusions suggested by this Treatise, may "yet perhaps," to adopt the modest words of the learned author of the *Rationale*, "be so sweetened as more readily to pardon those who, still abiding in their former judgments and being more confirmed hereby, do use THE ANCIENT FORM"; in holding fast to that Catholic tradition of the Reservation of the Blessed Sacrament, which with grateful hearts they devoutly cherish as a most precious inheritance in the Church of God.

Soli Deo Gloria.

www.ingramcontent.com/pod-product-compliance
Lightning Source LLC
Chambersburg PA
CBHW021734220426
43662CB00008B/841